LAST PLANE OUT OF SAIGON

LAST PLANE OUT OF SAIGON

Richard Pena
&
John Hagan

STORY MERCHANT BOOKS
BEVERLY HILLS
2014

2014
Story Merchant Books
9601 Wilshire Boulevard #1202
Beverly Hills CA 90210
http://www.storymerchant.com/books.html

Printed in the United States of America

Publisher's Cataloging-in-Publication data
Pena, Richard
Last Plane Out of Saigon / Richard Pena; with John Hagan.
p. cm.
ISBN 13: 978-0-9897154-1-6
ISBN 10: 0989715418
1. The main category of the book -History -Other category. 2. Another subject category -From one perspective. 3. More categories - And their modifiers. I. Johnson, Ben. II. Title.
HF0000.A0 A00 2010
299.000 00-dc22 2010999999

TABLE OF CONTENTS

FOREWORD

THE WALL
Richard Pena

RECENTLY THE TRAVELING WALL—A SMALLER REPLICA OF THE NATIONAL Vietnam Memorial in Washington, D.C.—came to my community in Austin, Texas. My wife Carolyn, whom I have known since before I went to Vietnam, thought that we should go visit it. For me, and many other Americans, viewing the Wall is an emotional and somber experience. This time was no different.

The Traveling Wall spanned the length of our local high school football field. We walked slowly past the etched names of all the soldiers who died or went missing in Vietnam. I saw one woman making a rubbing of one of the names with charcoal and a sheet of paper. For her, bringing the soldier closer in that way might have made the hurt a little more bearable. Seeing her tears, I knew that her pain had lasted for a very long time. "It will never go away," I thought to myself.

Loved ones had left all sorts of mementos and flowers by the memorial. There was even an old newspaper clipping of one soldier's death announcement. We slowly walked the length of the football field before turning back and revisiting the names a second time.

A young boy, about ten or twelve years old, walked towards us. He, too, was paying tribute to the fallen in his own way. By the look on his face, I could tell he was seeking some understanding from the memorial. He wore a red and black football jersey, the colors of the local high school. The school had recently won three state championships, and he must have been proud. One day, I thought, he might play on the team himself and maybe even compete in the state championship. I sighed and prayed that he would have the opportunity.

Each of the names represented a real loss. Carolyn wondered out loud what each person would have become, given the chance. She reflected on all the hopes and dreams that went unfulfilled because of the war, on what a waste it was—not just for the families, but for our country.

As we walked past the thousands of names—Donovan, Olson, Watson, Salinas, West, Yardoch, Neu, Viado, Stokes, Young, Torres, Spillner, Castle, Lopez, Zeller, Magee, Lafever—I felt only sorrow and regret. Most of these lives had been extinguished just as they were beginning. I no longer felt anger, for I had learned to accept this reality long ago. But like all the times I visited the Memorial in Washington, D.C., I felt as if I had been punched in the stomach.

In that moment of sadness, I wanted to reach out to those brave soldiers who died. What would they want now, some thirty-seven years after we left Vietnam? I feel they would want the truth to be told. It is for the sake of the 58,286 soldiers whose names are etched on the Wall, their families, the 3,100,000 soldiers who served in the Vietnam War—and, most of all, the truth—that John Hagan and I have pushed this book to publication.

While stationed in Vietnam as an operating room specialist, I kept a record of my wartime experiences and reflections. I left Vietnam on the final day of the American withdrawal, on one of the two very last planes out. Upon my return, I put the manuscript in a cardboard box, where it remained hidden away in the garage or attic for thirty-seven years. I knew that the American public had mostly overlooked the war, an important moment in their nation's history. But everyday responsibilities kept me busy, and I went on to quietly live my life. It wasn't until 2003, when I led a law delegation to Vietnam, that I realized the true significance of my departure on that final day.

Hanging on a wall of the War Remnants Museum in Ho Chi Minh City was a photo that depicted American troops boarding the final planes out of Vietnam. The inscription under the photo read, "Last Plane Out." Carolyn and I both immediately recognized a much younger me in the photo, carrying my law school briefcase. I had never seen this picture before. The Vietnamese consider this photograph to be one of the iconic images of the war, but to my knowledge the American public has been unaware of its existence.

Per the Paris Peace Accord signed January 23, 1973, America was to withdraw from Vietnam in sixty days. Those of us on the last two planes left on the sixty-first day. The American press was gone, the brass was gone—nearly everyone had left. I noticed a Viet Cong soldier taking a picture of us with a rudimentary camera. As I boarded the plane, I had a sense that someday the photo would surface.

Many Americans believe that the "end of the war" came in 1975 with the evacuation of the U.S. Embassy via helicopter. The photos of that event are deeply etched in our collective memory. However, historians know that American military involvement in the Vietnam War actually ended in March 1973 with the withdrawal of the last American combat troops. To this day, I am glad that I was one of the last ones out. At the time, I was relieved to know that no additional American soldiers would be sent to die for that war.

I would like to thank John Hagan for his tireless work—without him, this book would not have been possible. It was John who had me pull my manuscript from the attic and who understood its historical significance. The core of the book consists of journal entries I wrote while serving in Vietnam from 1972 to 1973.

I would like to thank the People To People Citizen Ambassador Programs for selecting me to lead the law delegation to Vietnam. Because of them, I was able to discover the Last Plane Out photo hanging in the American War Museums in Ho Chi Minh City. I thank the American Bar Foundation for its support and encouragement.

I would also like to thank my family and friends, who tried to understand and accept me back into "The World" when I returned. I would like to thank my wife, Carolyn Malley Pena, for her understanding, love, and support throughout these years. Above all, I would like to thank all those who continue to remember Vietnam and work to provide medical care for the veterans of all of our wars.

As you read the following pages, please understand that I wrote these words in real time as the war was happening. Stakes were high and emotions were raging. These are the truths as I experienced them.

Please remember, this is only an interpretation.
The truth, of course, is far stranger.

INTRODUCTION

FOR A MISTAKE?
John Hagan

JOHN KERRY ONCE ASKED WHICH YOUNG AMERICAN WOULD BE "THE LAST soldier to die for a mistake." Richard Pena knew that he did not want to be the answer. It was 1972, and the Vietnam War was still raging. Despite American troop withdrawals, the killing and dying continued unabated. Young and angry, Richard had no wish to accept a death sentence or prolong the inevitable American defeat. However, if he was going to serve in Vietnam, he wanted to be among the final American soldiers to leave—alive. As one of the last men out, he would bear many of the lasting lessons from this war.

In his youth, Richard learned to be proud of his country and his ability to find "his own way." He learned many valuable lessons through the compassionate discipline shown by his parents, Merced and Rebecca, as he was growing up. His parents and extended family, who were proud of their Hispanic heritage and values, taught him by example. Merced served in World War II and won a Silver Star for his service at Iwo Jima. Upon his return to San Antonio, Texas, he married Rebecca, his high school sweetheart and worked as a postman for the U.S. Postal Service, while Rebecca worked at Kelly Air Force Base. As rising middle-class parents of two baby boomer sons, they lived a version of the post-World War II American Dream.

15

Richard was born in 1948, fourteen months after his older brother, Mercy. Richard would never be tall, but he was fast. His father believed that Richard's speed and scrappiness would make him a basketball star, and he promised his son that there was "a way to win." Richard's mother would add, "There is always a way." In San Antonio, children played in the church leagues before moving on to middle school basketball. Richard's father put up a basketball hoop in the backyard and led the community effort to build a neighborhood church, which resulted in the Northwest Christian Church.

Eight-year-old Richard became a standout church-league player for Northwest Christian Church. When Richard was thirteen, he became starting guard for the basketball team at Horace Mann Junior High School and won several city championships. He later played on a high school team that was among the best in the city and in his senior year he received the best all-around athlete award. Richard's childhood friend, Fred Biery, still remembers a time when they played on opposite teams in their church league. One of Fred's exceptionally tall teammates played defense at half court and tried to stop Richard's dribble. To everyone's surprise, Richard dribbled through the legs of the tall defender and drove to the rim for a basket. "There is always a way."

Although his parents voted for Richard Nixon over John Kennedy in the 1960 presidential election, Richard hardly knew the difference between the candidates. His political awareness only emerged after the assassination of President Kennedy, and he became more politically engaged after he went off to college. In the fall of 1966, Richard enrolled at the University of Texas at Austin. The basketball coach, who had coached one of Richard's opponents in high school, wanted him to join the team as a walk-on. Richard declined, deciding to make schoolwork his priority instead.

The University of Texas at Austin was only seventy-five miles away from Richard's hometown, but the culture of the school made it seem worlds apart. During his undergraduate years, Richard became interested in the questions others were asking about American foreign policy. His interests took a bookish turn, and he abandoned sports completely in favor of economics and political science. The world was changing, too. Antiwar politics were on the march across America's campuses, and the University of Texas at Austin was no exception.

These were turbulent times. In 1966, draft card turn-ins and burnings attracted national attention. The fall of 1967—Richard's sophomore year—brought events like "Stop the Draft Week," the shutdown of the Draft Board in Oakland, and the first major Pentagon protest in Washington. The following year was stained by the assassinations of Dr. Martin Luther King Jr. and Robert Kennedy. Late that summer, the whole world watched as policemen rioted in Mayor Daley's Chicago and attacked antiwar demonstrators at the Democratic Party Convention.

The year 1968 became a wakeup call for Richard. The war had already killed nearly 40,000 U.S. soldiers by the time Lyndon Johnson returned to his Texas ranch to plan his presidential library on the Austin campus. Meanwhile, Hubert Humphrey became the Democrats' newly nominated war candidate, and the Vietnam War was in full swing as people were being drafted and killed. America was tearing itself apart. Richard started asking, "Why?"

The revelation of the My Lai massacre struck a raw nerve in Texas during Richard's senior year. A young journalist for the St. Louis Dispatch, Seymour Hersh, broke the explosive story that in March 1968 a twenty-six-year-old soldier, William Calley, deliberately led the mass slaughter of at least 109 Vietnamese civilian men, women, and children. Fuel was added to the fire when, in the spring of Richard's senior year, President Nixon announced the expansion of the war into Cambodia. Students roared into action in Austin and at over one hundred other university campuses throughout the United States. The American Council on Education estimated that there were nearly ten-thousand incidents of protest in 1969.

In May 1970, Austin antiwar leaders decided to hold a week-long protest. They planned to march across campus in order to avoid the need for a downtown parade permit, which the city had previously denied. The Monday before the march, word spread of nine wounded and four dead in Ohio. The young National Guardsmen who arrived at Kent State University had fatally shot the students with M-1 rifles recklessly loaded with live ammunition. The Crosby, Stills, Nash & Young song "Ohio" eulogized the dead students and later became a poignant call to arms.

By noon on Tuesday, 8,000 had gathered at the University of Texas at Austin to protest the Kent State shootings on the main campus mall. A crowd of 5,000 marched across the University and then headed downtown, disregarding the required permit. Richard participated in several campus demonstrations over the next week, some of which were reported in the national news media. Observers estimated that about half of all American university students took part in the May 1970 demonstrations. Richard ironically recalled that he held up a sign that read, "Hell No, We Won't Go." Only a few months later, he would be a soldier in Vietnam.

During another march in Austin that spring, a front line of demonstrators left campus and headed downtown into a phalanx of ten police officers. Followers fanned out around the initial melee. Five blocks on, the crowd encountered another twenty officers. The road of attack led to the state Capitol building, a symbol of government control in Austin. One student leader later gave an account of the event:

> By this point, the planners of the march were no longer in control. We had never left campus like that before; we all knew we wanted to go downtown. When we got to the Capitol, most of us went around. There were probably thirty armed police in riot gear and holding tear gas containers. . . . Some of the more militant people headed straight at the police. Fistfights broke out between police and students; some rocks were thrown. Four people were arrested. The police began firing tear gas. They went

absolutely nuts, even shooting off tear gas inside the Capitol as the students retreated toward campus. . . . A lot of people were blinded, being led by those who could still see. We were very inexperienced.[1]

Richard was among those young political protesters who were upset by all the wrongdoing and violence caused by the war. He viewed the marches as legitimate responses to the Kent State killings. To him, the Vietnam conflict was an illegitimate, politically motivated war that sacrificed young Americans without good reason. Those in power justified the war with the "domino effect" theory—that is, if the war was not fought, communism would spread like falling dominoes. Richard found the logic of this argument to be incoherent and disingenuous.

The week of protest in Austin snowballed into a general strike, and tens of thousands of students became involved in the rallies. The protesters even briefly took over the state Capitol. By Friday, students had completely abandoned classes in order to attend the strike. Governor Preston Smith, like governors in fifteen other states, called out the National Guard, and the city turned out 200 riot-equipped police. FBI agents with rifles lined the top of the clock tower as police helicopters swooped down over the campus.

During Friday's demonstration, 25,000 people came to protest the Cambodian invasion and the killings at Kent State. Led by a girl dressed in black, the march spanned thirteen blocks and featured a procession of American flags and coffins. As historian Beverly Burr writes, "The Friday march was the largest student protest activity to occur in Austin history, and has yet to be rivaled. The march turned into a huge love-in, which lasted into the twilight. That evening a memorial service for the four who were killed at Kent State was held on the main mall."[2] The demonstrations were a powerful continuation of the free speech and antiwar protests of the 1960s.

The historian Todd Gitlin concluded that the protests after the

Kent State shooting marked the peak of the student antiwar movement.[3] This may have been true for radicals on college campuses, but ordinary citizens everywhere were still being drafted into the military. Pro-war soldiers often became antiwar after being sent to Vietnam, and many servicemen were angry and motivated to halt the U.S. war effort. As the student movement broke off into factions, leadership of the antiwar initiative passed to veteran and active-duty soldiers.

Rebellious soldiers acted out in many ways. Some took part in agitation and protest, some went AWOL and deserted, while others succumbed to drugs. A few even took part in sabotage and mutiny.[4] The U.S. military effort was falling apart as the draft calls continued, albeit in smaller numbers. However, reports of declining draft quotas were of no consolation to those who actually received notices.

The winter and spring of 1970 solidified Richard's doubts about the necessity for the war. The militarized response to student protests, combined with the outspokenness of the soldiers who came home, made the prospect of military service odious. Richard's lottery number was in the 150s, which meant that he was nearly certain to receive a draft notice. In the spring of 1970, he was admitted into University of Texas School of Law, but the one-year educational deferment only delayed his vulnerability to the draft.

In 1971, John Kerry helped lead the Winter Soldier Investigation into atrocities committed during the war. Back from Vietnam, dressed in his soldier fatigues, Kerry reported the findings before the Senate Foreign Relations Committee. The day after he testified, Kerry joined thousands of veterans who threw their medals and ribbons over a fence in front of the U.S. Capitol. Kerry explained, "I'm not doing this for any violent reasons, but for peace and justice, and to try and make this country wake up once and for all."

Kerry's example struck a chord with Richard; the man had found a forceful way to both serve his country and challenge the war. A common chant against antiwar activists, "Love it or leave it!" suggested that dissenting opinions were not allowed. It implied that either you supported the war or you hated your country. Richard disagreed; he felt that citizens have a duty to speak up if they see something wrong. He believed that the greatest patriots are those who are willing to speak the uncomfortable truths.

Finally, Richard's draft notice arrived in the late spring of 1970. Like many draftees, he weighed his options. He agreed with the mainstream view that the war made no sense, but he also thought the war was wrong—morally wrong. Richard believed that the war was an immoral choice and not a moral necessity. However, the Selective Service Act and the local draft board blocked any legal attempt to escape the draft on moral grounds, so Richard had to try to figure a different way out.

When he appeared at his local draft board office in San Antonio, he was discouraged to see a plaque celebrating the high number of draftees they had inducted over the past month. Richard tried to fail his pre-induction physical by chugging Coca Colas to elevate his blood pressure. It didn't work. As they moved through the examination line, the person in front of him stepped forward and explained that he was deaf in one ear. The doctor simply asked how his hearing was in the other ear. Once the doctor declared the half-deaf draftee fit for service, Richard realized there was no escape.

Soon after his first year of law school, Richard's draft board ordered him to report for duty. He entered the Army on June 14, 1971.

The day before Richard reported for duty, the *New York Times* began publishing excerpts from the Pentagon Papers leaked by Defense Department employee Daniel Ellsberg. The papers revealed that the U.S. had secretly expanded bombing operations in Cambodia and Laos while engaging in clandestine coastal attacks on North Vietnam. This revelation further damaged the credibility of the Nixon administration. The Pentagon Papers also revealed that former President Johnson had already decided to expand the war in his 1964 race against Barry Goldwater—despite his campaign promises not to escalate the conflict.

Richard bypassed the option of attending Officer Candidate School, which might have kept him out of Vietnam but would have lengthened his military service commitment. He wanted to minimize his obligation by only serving two years—even if it meant going to Vietnam while the war was still being fought. Congress abandoned the draft several months before the conclusion of his tour of duty, making Richard one of the last Americans drafted into service for Vietnam (and any other war since).

When Richard entered the Army, many active soldiers and veterans were resisting the war through writing, speeches, and protest actions. Both the public and the military had begun to think of the Vietnam War as a mistake. At one point, more than 250 antiwar newspapers circulated through U.S. military bases and off-base coffee houses.

As the departure date drew closer, Richard prepared himself for his mission with greater clarity of purpose. He decided not to become romantically involved before going to Vietnam, feeling that a long-distance relationship would be unfair to the other person. He wanted to confine the damage to himself as much as possible, knowing that he could be among those killed.

Richard assumed the war would be hard but could scarcely imagine what it would actually be like. Once in Vietnam, he decided to document his experiences in writing. He had no formal literary training and didn't see himself as Ernest Hemingway or Norman Mailer, but he wanted to immerse himself and create a truthful record of the war. Perhaps by writing about Vietnam in a way that others could not, he could provide a unique perspective. In any case, he knew that he had a story that needed to be told.

Written as the Vietnam War was ending in death and defeat, this book is the result of his efforts. After Richard returned from Vietnam, the manuscript sat unread in his garage and attic for more than three decades—an untold story about the final, painful year of a war that most wanted to forget.

In 2003, Richard led a delegation of lawyers to Vietnam as part of a People to People Citizen Ambassador Program. In Ho Chi Minh City, he visited the War Remnants Museum—formerly the Museum of American War Crimes. One of the fellow delegates knew that Richard left Vietnam on the last day of American involvement. Once they were inside the museum, the delegate noticed a photo and told Richard to take a look.

The Vietnamese had labeled the photo, *Last Plane Out.* Richard was shocked to recognize himself in the picture as one of the Americans boarding a plane. He took his wife Carolyn, a co-leader of the delegation, and asked, "What do you see?"

Without hesitation, she said, "That's you getting on the plane."

The picture was of Richard, thirty years earlier, climbing the steps to the plane that flew him out of Vietnam. Carolyn not only recognized Richard, she even recognized his law school briefcase, which he carried in Vietnam and for years afterwards.

The jarring experience led him to reconsider the significance of his manuscript. Like the war, his writing had been neglected and forgotten. Fortunately, when he returned to Austin, the manuscript was still in a brown cardboard box in the attic, exactly as he had left it. Since his return from the war, the manuscript had traveled with him from house to house and garage to garage. For the last fifteen years, it had sat untouched in his attic.

Richard's tour in Vietnam lasted from May 1972 through the end of March 1973. This book contains his actual writings from that year. Before each group of entries, I provide historical and political context for the "real time" in which his experiences took place.

There is an underlying tone of bitterness in this work, but remember that these were very bitter times. Above all else, the reader should know that all of the events related in this book actually happened and that Richard's feelings and emotions were likewise entirely real. History has confirmed Richard's beliefs and observations. As Robert McNamara lamented, "Yet we were wrong, terribly wrong. We owe it to future generations to explain why."[5]

There are many books about Vietnam, but the approach and visceral reality of *Last Plane Out of Saigon* is unique. Richard's thoughts and experiences are his own, but they are something that all Vietnam veterans can identify with. As an operating room specialist, he saw the bloody consequences of the war in graphically human terms. Richard has given us eyewitness evidence of the terrible mistake that was the Vietnam War.

Richard describes the last frantic days before the American military withdrawal from Vietnam. After the Army honorably discharged him, awarding him the National Defense Service Medal, the Army Commendation Medal and the Vietnam Service Medal, among other decorations, he returned to law school. In May 1976, he received his Doctor of Jurisprudence Degree from the University of Texas School of Law, and the State Bar of Texas admitted Richard to the practice of law on November 1, 1976. His work in the legal realm is also a part of this story.

The Richard Pena who returned from Vietnam was a very different man from the teenager who had arrived at the University of Texas as an undergraduate seven years earlier. This book is a real-time account of the anger, resistance, and resilience that developed from his wartime experiences.

"This unnecessary war was unconstitutionally commenced by the President, who may be telling us the truth—but not the whole truth. He has swept the war on and on in showers of blood. His mind, taxed beyond its powers, is running like some tortured creature on a burning surface. Stop this war Mr. President. For the love of God, stop this war."
—Robert Edwin Lee and Jerome Lawrence,
The Night Thoreau Spent in Jail

PART I

JUST THE BEGINNING
John Hagan

FOR MANY AMERICANS, THE VIETNAM WAR IS LITTLE MORE THAN A BLUR. As Henry Kissinger writes in *Ending the Vietnam War*, "Vietnam has become the black hole of American historical memory."[6] Memories of the last year of the conflict are especially hazy in the public mind. This is partly because of the collective exhaustion the nation felt during those desperate days of defeat, but a great deal of information about the war was also suppressed or went unreported.

In 1970, Le Duc Tho of North Vietnam's politburo and then-Secretary of State Henry Kissinger began a series of on-and-off peace negotiations. Meanwhile, George McGovern and others in Congress tried to end the war by mandating the withdrawal of U.S. forces. The Nixon Administration resisted, but Congress successfully forced troop withdrawals from the region during this period. This marked the beginning of what Nixon called the "Vietnamization" of the conflict, as military responsibilities were shifted onto the South Vietnamese government. The question was whether the South Vietnamese forces could stand and fight alone.

Just days before Richard boarded his plane in May 1972 in Oakland, CA, President Nixon announced the next round of troop withdrawals, completing a 70,000 reduction announced three months earlier. From the peak commitment of 545,000, only about 65,000 American troops were in Vietnam when Richard arrived. Before he was deployed, he kept hearing a tantalizing rumor that their deployment would be canceled. This was not to be.

Soon after Richard's plane full of G.I.s landed in Saigon, the Nixon Administration announced that no more draftees would be sent to Vietnam. The massive traffic of conscripts and volunteer soldiers began to flow in the opposite direction: from "The Nam" back into "The World."

A week before Richard's plane touched down in the famously stifling heat and humidity of Tan Son Nhut Airbase near Saigon, North Vietnam launched a major offensive that threatened to abruptly overthrow the South Vietnamese government. Because it began six months before the 1972 U.S. presidential election, the timing of the attack echoed the Tet Offensive—the North Vietnamese onslaught that led Lyndon Johnson to abandon his reelection hopes in 1968. Back then, Walter Cronkite famously sounded the alarm: "What the hell is going on? I thought we were winning this war!" Nobody, Nixon and Kissinger in particular, could miss the parallel.

Several divisions of North Vietnamese (NVA) troops launched a three-wave attack: the first across the northern Demilitarized Zone into Quang Tri province; the second into the Central Highlands of South Vietnam; and the third towards An Loc, a provincial capital of about 20,000 persons just fifty miles from Saigon. The NVA wiped out nearly half of the South Vietnamese 22nd Division in the Central Highlands. When Kissinger met with Le Duc Tho in Paris, An Loc was surrounded and under siege by NVA troops. It seemed South Vietnam was near collapse.

Richard arrived at the 3rd Field Hospital in Saigon during the North Vietnamese siege of An Loc, which lasted from May to July 1972. Officers in the First Airborne Brigade reported that they had never seen such a sustained application of firepower. The North

Vietnamese shot down four U.S. aircraft and managed to kill most of the residents of An Loc as they fled from their destroyed homes.

South Vietnamese President Thieu was determined to defend An Loc "at all costs," and he committed many of his best forces to the battle. Having withdrawn most of its combat troops by 1972, the United States supported the South Vietnamese by unleashing its remaining air power in full force, although it stopped short of using nuclear weapons. The NVA suffered heavy losses from the bombardment and failed to take the town.

By midsummer, there was no An Loc left to win. The artillery assault reduced the town to rubble and turned its surviving residents into refugees. A reporter for *Time* magazine described what was left of An Loc two months after the battle to save it began:

> There are perhaps six buildings left in the town, none with a solid roof. There is no running water or electricity. Every street is shattered by artillery craters and littered with the detritus of a battle that saw a bit of every kind of war. Everywhere you walk you hear the crackle of shifting shell fragments when you put your foot down.[7]

The same *Time* reporter concluded that:

> . . . for the foreseeable future, An Loc is dead—as dead as the hundreds of North Vietnamese who were caught in the city's northern edge by U.S. bombing, and whose putrefaction makes breathing in An Loc so difficult when the afternoon breeze comes up. Perhaps the best that can be said is that the city died bravely, and that—in a year that included the fall of Quang Tri and Tan Canh—is no small achievement.[8]

More than 10,000 civilian refugees—who had lived underground for two months to survive the siege—fled the city on foot and headed for camps near Chon Thanh. Nobody knows how many of the An Loc refugees died on Highway 13 or in the camps, but it is likely that nearly all of them perished.

Many have claimed that the U.S. and South Vietnamese won the battle for An Loc, but this is a mistaken assessment of tragic proportions. An Loc was a hollow victory, and the South Vietnamese eventually had to abandon all their bases in the province. The battle revealed how dependent the South Vietnamese military was on American air power, and the strategy of "Vietnamization" was shown to have failed. Congress reduced U.S. funding for combat activities in Vietnam and eventually cut funding altogether.

In a televised January 1972 speech, Nixon revealed that secret peace negotiations had occurred in Paris. The revelation raised hopes that the war would soon end. The day before Richard Pena flew to Vietnam, Henry Kissinger met with Le Duc Tho in Paris.

Nixon and Kissinger decided that, "the back of the North Vietnamese offensive had to be broken militarily." [9] Nixon demanded that the U.S. withdraw from Vietnam with the upper hand, which became his operational definition of "peace with honor." In his mind, it was the only way to ensure that the world would remain stable and democracy would survive.

Thirty years later, secret Oval Office tape recordings—made during the same week that Richard Pena arrived in Vietnam—were uncovered in which Nixon proposed using nuclear weapons in the region. On February 28, 2002, *USA Today* reported the following:

> "I'd rather use the nuclear bomb," Nixon told Kissinger, his national security adviser, a few weeks before he ordered a major escalation of the Vietnam War. "That, I think, would just be too much," Kissinger replied softly in his baritone voice, in a conversation uncovered among 500 hours of Nixon tapes released Thursday. Nixon responded matter-

of-factly. "The nuclear bomb. Does that bother you?" he asked. Then he closed the subject by telling Kissinger: "I just want you to think big." He also said "I don't give a damn" about civilians killed by U.S. bombing.

Instead, Nixon ordered the military to bomb North Vietnamese urban areas as well as the dikes controlling floodwater in the north. A few days after Richard's arrival in Vietnam, Nixon gave a nationally televised speech in which he announced the beginning of "Operation Linebacker." The operation involved dropping naval mines in North Vietnam's Haiphon harbor and other ports, along with intensified bombings of roads, bridges, and oil facilities.

U.S. and South Vietnamese forces also intensified their bombings in the south. In one attack, a South Vietnamese plane napalmed a village, burning a number of civilians alive. This attack resulted in the famous photograph of nine-year-old Phan Thi Kim Phuc, naked and horribly burned, running down a road in a screaming panic as she fled from the attack. This image, as well as filmed footage of the event, formed a searing memory that forever turned public opinion against the war.

George McGovern responded to the mining, bombing, killing, and maiming by insisting, "The President must not have a free hand in Indochina any longer. . . . The nation cannot stand it. The Congress must not allow it. . . . The political regime in Saigon is not worth the loss of one more American life."

A week and a half later, Nixon and Kissinger met in the Roosevelt Room of the White House with seven presidents of Ivy League universities. The university presidents lamented the casualties and destructiveness of a war made "for reasons that are not clear and that no one seems willing to defend." One worried that, "I don't see how we can continue to run our universities if the war escalates. . . . What will we face in September?"[10]

After his nationally televised speech—in the same month that he privately considered a nuclear attack—Nixon wrote Kissinger a memo urging him "to look for new ways of hurting the enemy with air-power." Nixon declared, "We have the power to destroy [North Vietnam's] war-making capacity. The only question is whether we have the will to use that power. What distinguishes me from Johnson is that I have the *will* in spades."[11]

In his book, Kissinger proclaimed that this was "one of the finest hours of Nixon's presidency." He believed the force of Nixon's air and naval attacks paved the way for "an honorable withdrawal," and that they were essential to "the entire postwar design of American foreign policy."[12] However, Kissinger's logic is impossible to square with the loss of life, the slow-motion collapse of the South Vietnamese government, the meaninglessness of the war for subsequent American foreign policy, and the evolution of the peaceful trade relationship between American and Vietnam that prospers today.

Nixon's massive bombing campaign—using more than 200 B-52s and mining North Vietnam's harbors—temporarily succeeded in stalling the NVA's 1972 spring offensive. Negotiations resumed in the summer, with the possibility of an agreement in August. The proposal envisioned a South Vietnamese coalition government composed fifty–fifty of both communists and non-communists. Kissinger took the agreement to President Nguyen Van Thieu in Saigon, but Thieu was unwilling to share power under those terms and rejected the proposal.

By the end of August, the U.S. had drawn down its forces to fewer than 30,000 men —Richard Pena among them. Thieu was clearly concerned that his government would not survive if the Americans withdrew or if he was forced into a power-sharing arrangement. Despite his desire for "peace with honor," Nixon didn't seem to care much about the long-term survival of an independent South Vietnamese government. He wanted Kissinger to reach a reconciliation agreement with Le Duc Tho as soon as possible. Nixon told Kissinger that if an agreement was made, Kissinger should return to Saigon to "cram it down [Thieu's] throat."[13]

In late October, the American electorate faced a choice between Nixon and McGovern. Kissinger believed he had the elements of an acceptable peace agreement, but he returned to Saigon to find President Thieu even less cooperative than before. On October 22, 1972, after concluding his meetings with Thieu in Saigon, Kissinger telegraphed Washington with an unambiguous message: "Thieu has just rejected the entire plan or any modification of it and refuses to discuss any further negotiations on the basis of it."[14] The upcoming election made it difficult for Nixon to bully Thieu the way he had before; if Thieu's resistance was exposed, the American public would see it as the tail wagging the dog.

It is doubtful that President Nixon needed an agreement to end the war in order to win the election against George McGovern. Nixon was still far ahead in the polls, despite the unfinished Vietnam conflict and gradual emergence of the Watergate scandal. Despite Nixon's worry about Kissinger's foreign accent, he told Kissinger to hold a news conference announcing the peace prospects. Kissinger met the press on October 26, 1972, and boasted, "We believe that peace is at hand." It was a remarkable overstatement, if not an outright lie.

After Nixon's landslide victory over George McGovern, it became obvious that Thieu had unequivocally rejected Kissinger's peace agreement. Now unencumbered by electoral politics, Nixon and Kissinger decided once again to bombard North Vietnam into submission. They believed that unleashing B-52 bombers over the northern part of North Vietnam would produce a "shock effect" that would lead to victory.[15] Officially codenamed "Operation Linebacker II," their plan led to the infamous twelve-day "Christmas bombing" campaign against North Vietnam. Much of Congress and the press took the view that the United States was intentionally killing civilians as part of a targeted campaign of terror.

Richard Pena served in Saigon throughout this intense and contradictory period of optimistic peace talks and massive bombing attacks. He spent the Christmas of 1972 in the 3rd Field Hospital, the last U.S. military hospital remaining in Vietnam. The war had been resurrected in all its futile fury, and its dead and wounded flowed ceaselessly through the operating room where Richard worked.

There is much that has been said about Vietnam;
there is much more that can only be understood
by those of us who were there.

LEAVING "THE WORLD"
Richard Pena, Summer 1972

THESE ACCOUNTS AND INTERPRETATIONS ARE NOT WRITTEN FOR NOTORIETY nor out of boredom. There is a story here in Vietnam that must be told. It goes beyond the farce and political tragedy that American involvement in this country has come to represent. It has nothing to do with the causes or mistakes that led to our involvement; rather it deals with the human consequences of those policies. The world must see how little consideration is being given to the people whose homes are being destroyed and who we "are protecting." Indeed, can history ever reflect the contempt that those responsible deserve for what they have done here? Our nation must also see what it has done to our sons and daughters, and in the end, the destruction it has set in motion for itself.

I begin these accounts after having been in Vietnam for two months. Only now, after long months have passed, have I overcome my initial disbelief of this apparent madness. How distant this is from law school, from the concepts of justice, fair play, and logical reasoning. Soon after I was drafted, I was to find that there is little justice, fair play and logic in the military. There is even less in this war.

In the beginning, I attempted to ignore the people of this country and their stories. I attempted to isolate myself in a bubble in order to prevent myself from being affected by this war. A goal, common to us here, is to survive 365 days and then retake our place in American society. However, no one who is or was in this forsaken land will ever return home the same. Nor should that be anyone's wish. Those who are fortunate to return home with their physical qualities intact can better conceal the scars and imprints left by this war. However, they will never forget. Nor will the hundreds of thousands who return home as shattered specimens. Then there are those who return to America only to be housed in the mental wards of Veteran's Hospitals. They also bear the scars of Vietnam. They are the ones who cannot forget.

It is to these men and women that the following pages are dedicated.

THE DEBATE
Richard Pena, Summer 1972

THE DEBATE WHICH THE VIETNAM FIASCO HAS PROMPTED, IS BOTH DIFFICULT and necessary. Was America justified in its intervention in this small country? Has Vietnam been an accident, an abortive attempt at containing a concept called communism? Can America win in Vietnam? It now appears that many of the difficulties in Vietnam have turned out to be theoretical failures; most of our theories about Vietnam, the military as well as political ones, have proven to be wrong. But in the endless debates about this war, the scholars, the politicians, and the military all base their opinions on a concept that victory makes right. These pages are not an attempt to resolve the debate, but rather to reveal that any assumption of merit attached to this intervention is far outweighed by the tragedies and horrors that Vietnam has prompted.

Americans began dying in Vietnam in 1961, and eleven years later, they are still dying here. This has been, by far, the longest war that American sons and daughters have been forced to die in. Yet the debate continues, with the debaters apparently unwilling to see that the "rightness" or "wrongness" of this war has now become academic. But they are not the ones who have seen the toll this war has taken in human terms. They have not seen tens of thousands of refugees marching homeless from their destructed homes. They have not watched as an American soldier, with the physique of a varsity athlete, had his leg amputated. They have not held that leg once it was detached, and wondered if this was not a page from the insanity depicted in *Catch 22.*

But perhaps greater than this, they have not had to lose a son or daughter, or faced death themselves in this forsaken land. It is not so much the fear of death that haunts one in Vietnam, but the fear of dying for a policy dictated out of ignorance and falsehoods. Yet the debate continues, with the participants unaware that they are discussing a moot question. How can there be a rightness to this war? Surely not because of SEATO, "collective defense," Article 51 of the U.N. Charter, or the Dulles concept of the domino theory. These have long been recognized either as misconceptions or as vain attempts to justify American intervention in the civil strife of Vietnam.

Policy makers and administrators could only be partially condemned if their only error was a lack of foresight. However, far greater moral crimes are being charged by those of us who have been made to suffer in Vietnam. A president and his policy makers have a right to gamble with their own political fortunes, but they have no right to seek these fortunes at the expense of the innocent, slaughtered and maimed in a small country halfway around the world.

At the time of this writing, American troops are being withdrawn. It is very possible that this war will be resolved by November '72. Yet this "timely" withdrawal can only be seen as a political maneuver aimed at re-election by the present administration. This administration is merely accomplishing now what it could have done the first months it was in office. But that would not have "ensured" re-election in 1972.

As a result, more than 20,000 Americans have died during the reign of this administration. Many more have become POW's or MIA's. Countless more will never be able to retake their place in society. How will they explain to their friends why they cannot walk, or see, or laugh? How can America live with the destruction that it has implemented on the innocent of this land? Very simply, it will not be told the truth.

Yet this administration is but one in a long line responsible for this nightmare. Make no mistake, this nightmare is very real to those of us who came to Vietnam. We are the ones who cannot turn the war off after the six o'clock news. Doesn't America wonder what makes an American soldier, sworn to defend his nation, become a radical Vietnam veteran against the war? Perhaps someday our nation will put partisanship aside and unite behind the resolution that there must never be another Vietnam. This it must do if it is to survive.

THE ARRIVAL
Richard Pena, Summer 1972

MY PLANE LANDED IN VIETNAM IN EARLY MAY OF '72. AS I STEPPED OFF the plane, I was slapped with the hotness and humidity of the night. My mind was racing back to the friends, the loved ones I had left at home. It was as if I'd suddenly stepped onto an entirely different plane of reality. Only later would I realize that there was no sanity in my new world, only madness.

I had come to Vietnam at a very bad time, both chronologically and militarily. Chronologically, future textbooks would classify me as one of the last draftees to be sent to 'Nam. Militarily, the situation could not have been worse. There was serious doubt whether South Vietnam would stand another two weeks. In fact, there was serious speculation that my plane would bypass Saigon because by our arrival time it would already be in North Vietnamese hands.

The long-planned "Vietnamization" policy was a catastrophe. On Easter Sunday, the North Vietnamese had launched an unprecedented invasion against the South. Just as the world was envisioning a winding down, a settlement, peace, the Vietnamese people were once again paying an awful price. South Vietnamese refugees fled in masses ahead of the oncoming North Vietnamese. Young ARVN (Army of the Republic of Vietnam) troops were throwing down their weapons and fleeing with the villagers. Several weeks later the Saigon government

41

imposed mandatory haircut regulations to ensure that males could not disguise themselves as women—as many had done in this retreat.

The situation was extremely bleak for the South Vietnamese Army. They were being routed on every front. The South Vietnamese had abandoned the capital of Quang Tri. Hue received the burden of many of these refugees. The looting and burning of Hue added to the increasing aura of impending disaster. Refugees and army deserters swelled the population of Hue from 150,000 to 350,000.

On every front the same thing was happening. South Vietnamese soldiers were throwing down their arms and clothing and were fleeing with the refugee horde. North Vietnamese troops laid siege to An Loc, a town 60 miles from Saigon. The United States provided air support in an unprecedented quantity. Yet this did little to deter the onslaught of the North Vietnamese.

It was in this setting that I first set foot in Vietnam. Amid growing concern for our welfare, I groped for the rapidly diminishing hope that I would someday return to my homeland. Although I was aware that much would happen in the intermediate 365 days, I could not even begin to conceive of the actual impact that this Vietnam experience was to produce. As I stepped off the plane, I could not help but wonder why I had been sentenced to exile in this forsaken land.

"They created a desert and called it peace."
—Tacitus

MASS CASUALTIES
Richard Pena, Summer 1972

THE AMERICAN PUBLIC FINDS HUMOR IN *MASH*. THOSE WHO HAVE SEEN
the truth of Vietnam see a depiction of war that sometimes comes
close to showing reality.

Earlier this month, the hospital was put on alert for 200–300 mass
casualties, which were supposed to arrive within twenty-four hours.
The entire hospital was frantic in an attempt to prepare for the incom-
ing casualties. The patients at the hospital were all evacuated to the
Philippines and Japan. Many more beds were brought in. Everywhere
one looked, even in the courtyard, litters were set up. Blood was flown
in from Japan.

Further news revealed that the causalities were refugees from An
Loc. The siege had finally been broken. Many had been wounded for
two months. Also, there were not 200, but 2,000. How, a rational man
must ask himself, did the Army expect to accommodate all of those
casualties in a hundred-bed hospital? The absurdity was compounded
when it was learned that the refugees were marching the sixty miles
from An Loc.

A week later the casualties had not arrived. The end result, as
could be expected, was a comedy of tragic errors. The casualties were
forced to march over Highway 13—which was Communist held. En
route, they were mortared by the Communists. Many died as a result.

We were also told others were killed when the American B-52s, which were providing air support by bombing ahead of the marching horde, accidentally dropped their bombs on the marchers. Not a single marcher got through to the hospital.

Around this same time, our side was napalming fifteen miles south of Saigon. The Air Force accidentally missed the North Vietnamese, who were the original targets, and wiped out an ally South Vietnamese village!

The tragedy in Vietnam sometimes bordered on horrified amusement because of the unbelievable stupidity.

Part II

In Country
John Hagan

BEFORE THEIR FINAL 1954 DEFEAT AT DIEN BIEN PHU, THE FRENCH imagined that Saigon would become the "Paris of the East" or the "Paris of the Orient." This was long before Richard's arrival and the American occupation of South Vietnam. In the wartime reporting of the Vietnam War, references are often made to the French occupation, a time that many remembered with a moody mixture of nostalgia and regret. The villa that Richard and his fellow medics settled into during their stay in Saigon was a carryover from this earlier era.

In the early 1950s, during what seemed to be a period of colonial success, a French general, Jean Marie de Lattre, established and briefly held a number of fortified positions from Hanoi to the Gulf of Tonkin known as the "De Lattre Line." In Graham Greene's 1955 novel *The Quiet American*, a Vietnamese detective warns the British protagonist about the illusion of security during this period:

> You're a journalist. You know better than I do that we can't
> win. . . . We were nearly beaten in '50. De Lattre has given
> us two years of grace—that's all. But we are professionals:
> we have to go on fighting till the politicians tell us to stop.

Probably they will get together and agree to the same peace
that we could have had at the beginning, making nonsense
of all these years.[16]

Greene's fictional detective imagined a scenario eerily similar to
the one Kissinger and Nixon would play out as they negotiated the
American exit nearly two decades later in 1973. However, American
policymakers failed to heed this lesson, and they went on to repeat the
same blunders on an even greater scale.

Richard Pena witnessed the end of this mistake as he arrived in
Saigon during the last year of Vietnam's "American War." Although in
earlier years it only held around 500,000 people, at that time Saigon burst
with a population well over three million. The city overflowed with
refugees who had fled the violence caused by all parties—the North and
South Vietnamese armies, the Viet Cong, and the American forces.

By 1972, after pushing literally millions of soldiers through
Vietnam, the American war machine was winding down the effort and
gradually withdrawing the remaining combat troops. However,
Nixon's massive and expanded fleet of B-52s conducted saturation
bombing campaigns with a new intensity across much of the airspace
in both the south and the north.

Newcomers to Saigon often confused the distant rumbling of
bombing runs with the thunder of the city's rainstorms. The largesse
of the military stoked the overheated and chaotic character of the city.
The scorching sun competed with drenching monsoons, but neither
ever seemed to slow the tumult of traffic along Saigon's Tu Do Street.

Polluting fumes spewed from the multitude of vehicles and motor
scooters. Motorcycles, motorbikes, and pedal rickshaws swarmed in a
constant stream of traffic, zooming past antiquated buses and battered
Renaults and Citroens left over from the French occupation. Whole
families balanced precariously on all manner of foot-pedaled and
modestly motorized conveyances. The traffic was governed only by
the unpredictable rules of the street.

The war had tightened around Saigon like a noose. The rising death toll crushed any hope of return to the nostalgic luxury that some still associated with the hotels on Tu Do Street. Those dreams had vanished in the 1950s, when Vietnam might have still hoped to become a coveted colony of Old Europe.

By the late 1960s, Saigon instead was characterized by a raucous and kinetic energy. Teenage prostitutes angled for customers from the doorways, street corners, and hazily lit bars of Tu Do Street as street merchants aggressively pushed black-market wares. Amputees of all ages hobbled along, a constant reminder of the bombs, mines, and primitive medicine practiced outside the U.S. military hospitals. Women carefully navigated the hazardous avenues dressed in thin pajama trousers, shaded hats, and sandals.

The business of Saigon's streets continued long into the deceptively languid evenings, and the nights that followed were full of danger and sleaze. Looking out onto the horizon from the tops of Saigon's tall buildings, one could see the flashes and firestorms of America's deadly and hopeless war; it all began anew each morning.

These images and memories of wartime Saigon live on not only in novels and photos, but also on Internet sites such as "Déjà vu Vietnam."[17] This website was developed by veterans who returned to Saigon to photograph the streets and create guided audio tours of famous landmarks from the era.

During their service, American soldiers frequently visited the USO building on Tu Do Street. At the USO, homesick soldiers could place phone calls back to "The World" from which they were now so far removed. John Ketwig, a G.I. in Vietnam, described his feelings of longing and loneliness: "Everyone dreamed about The World, talked about The World, cried about The World. There was nothing more important. The World wasn't a planet. It was your hometown, your tree-lined street in the suburbs, your tenement in the ghetto."[18]

Most of the soldiers hoped to return to "The World," if only they could survive their time in Vietnam. However, Ketwig recalled the disappointment of his first visit to the USO building: "The sidewalk was crowded. This was the land of opportunity for Saigon's beggars, and I burst into the USO to escape their outstretched hands. Now that I was here, I was in no real hurry to call home. I had five hours, and what should I say?"[19]

Ketwig discovered that the phone system was jury-rigged by volunteer ham-radio operators. The tense, emotional conversations he overheard were stilted and awkward because each phrase had to end with the word "stop." When Ketwig finally made his own call home, he found that he was unable to communicate with his family in a meaningful way. Despite its good intentions, the USO could only put a gloss over the soldiers' fear of death and misfortune; it was a massively insufficient salve for all the transient and destructive emotions of America's military involvement in Vietnam.

American soldiers in Vietnam soon learned to look elsewhere for places of refuge. For Richard, it was the villa that he and his friends rented a few blocks from the 3rd Field Hospital. Though not nearly as posh or exotic as the name might suggest, the villas of Saigon were an escape from the misery and olive drab monotony of the military machine. Electricity was fitful, rats and insects outnumbered the human tenants, bathrooms were moldy, and water sometimes ran rusty from the taps. Still, life at the villa meant relaxation and friendship—evoking distant, happier memories of "The World" left behind. The time Richard spent there was a respite from the grim isolation and physical toll of the otherwise suffocating wartime violence.

The villa's atmosphere was by no means entirely benign. The alliance with the South Vietnamese government was tainted by suspicion and fear, and the Americans were occupiers of the city every bit as much as they were its defenders. The Viet Cong remained an unseen but feared presence. Barbed wire surrounded the villa and hung over the edge of the porches to ward off attacks.

Yet Richard and the other Americans who occupied the villa felt far safer there than among the crowds of Saigon or during the walk to and from the hospital. On the right day, in the right weather and with the right group of friends, the villa was a release, a social and psychological escape to a far more pleasant mental space.

Richard and the other American soldiers who lived in the villa often gathered on the veranda—which they nicknamed "The Beach"—to watch the life of the street below. Some would smoke pot and drink beer to numb themselves from the horrors of war. When Richard and his friend Randy got tired of just watching, they would dive into the streets of Saigon, taking their refreshments along for a ride in one of the ubiquitous pedicabs.

Saigon's neighborhoods were famous for their variety. The old Chinese neighborhood of Cholon was a reminder of Vietnam's deep and enduring regional ties, which the American arrivals often had difficulty appreciating. As Richard and Randy rode along the streets of Cholon, they got glimpses of a world far beyond their understanding, in a city that nonetheless was fast becoming a defining part of their lives.

Richard's group spent their happiest evenings simply hanging out on the veranda. Since they lived several floors above an Asian restaurant, their thoughts frequently turned to food and drink. A favorite ploy was to tie a rope to a bucket and lower it over the edge of the veranda to the restaurant below. They would then yell down their order for grilled cheese sandwiches and a round of gin and tonics. The song they blasted from that balcony in the summer of '72 featured Alvin Lee playing blues guitar with his band, Ten Years After, at Woodstock. The refrain of the song improbably but happily insisted, "I'm going home."

"If you have a farm in Vietnam
And a house in hell
Sell the farm
And go home"
—Michael Casey, "A Bummer"

THE VILLA
Richard Pena, Summer 1972

WE DO NOT LIVE IN VIETNAM—WE EXIST. HOW CAN I DESCRIBE THESE days of existence when the war has already been acknowledged as a fiasco? Vietnam is no longer called the Southeast Theater, for it has long ago become the Theater of the Absurd. Most American soldiers here act out their various roles, regardless of how illogical and insane, in the hope that the 365 days will soon be over. However, each day is so long, so significant, that we refer to them as "Year Long Days."

We have our work in the operating room to occupy many of the hours, but none of us can ever forget where we are—we can never forget our homes. A day never goes by without someone bringing up The World, which is what we call America. A minute does not pass without us thinking of it. Instantly, we flash back to little things that seem insignificant to many people—a car ride, a hot bath, a McDonald's hamburger. Words like "civilization," "morality," "justice," and "love" are merely remembered as representations of philosophies that are said to exist. It is these memories of what once was, and perhaps a childlike anticipation of what will someday be, that keep us going throughout these long days.

There are some who were not strong enough to cope with the bad hand they had been dealt by fate. They cannot see a tomorrow, perhaps because most of them did not have much of a yesterday. These are the ones who turn to "scag" (heroin) and eventually end up at DETOX (Drug Rehabilitation Center) or with a 212 Discharge (less than honorable).

Others accept their assignments and are content merely to be alive. These are the ones who live, work, and seldom leave the confines of the hospital. They justify it by saying that they are saving money. These two types of people are the ones who easily submit and accept defeat. To the latter, Vietnam is simply a bad experience, which they will tolerate for 365 days and then return home.

Others are not made to fit into either of these molds. My spirit is too restless, too inquisitive. I have to know more about this war by knowing the people. I have to know what they feel, what they want, and why. After all, we have come halfway around the globe to defend them.

In short, I am determined to learn what cannot be taught through textbooks. By gaining knowledge which few have the opportunity to learn, by expanding my individual consciousness, I am determined to make Vietnam a positive page in my life. It is for this reason that I felt possessed to move out into the Vietnamese community, and I immediately accepted the opportunity to move into a villa with five other OR techs. As Brother Leary very aptly put it, "You owe it to yourself."

I am astonished by the opportunity that is before me. I have been put in such a unique position. Being assigned to the 3rd Field Hospital is a stroke of luck. We at 3rd Field see a completely different side of war than anyone else in Vietnam. 3rd Field is not a military post, but rather an individual hospital within the Saigon area. As a result, we are not bombarded with the usual barrage of military regulations. Although we seldom see the actual jungle combat of the war, we do see the results of the war in human terms, and we do see the war that is fought in the city. This refers not only to the mangled and maimed brought into the emergency room and operating room, but also to the effect the war has on Vietnamese people.

Rev, one of my many roommates, once brought home a soldier

who was assigned at Long Binh. His eyes seemed dazed; he appeared to be in a mild state of shock. "I've been in country for six months," he said amazingly, "and this is the first time I've actually been out with the people. Hell, I haven't even been off post in six months. What are they like?"

A July Saturday in Vietnam
Richard Pena, Summer 1972

THIS HAD BEEN A DREARY SATURDAY. I LAY AROUND ALL DAY. I HAD EARLIER planned on getting much accomplished today, but somehow those plans seemed to have fallen by the wayside. I had managed to become settled in my new "summer villa," which I was sharing with five other OR techs.

For some reason I was intoxicated with the Vietnamese this Saturday. I had earlier gone down the street to the market. There I was viewed with suspicious curiosity, probably as an American looking at and mocking their way of life. An old lady was selling fish and shrimp that reeked as if spoiled. Another was selling some type of reddish Asian fruit. The flies and mud seemed indistinguishable from the goods. An old man was pushing a three-wheeled cart, announcing his wares with a loud proclamation. Little boys and girls were playing in the narrow, filthy street.

They were apparently unaware of the drama of which they were a part. All were completely dedicated and involved with the proceedings of the day. Later they would go home and count the few piasters (Vietnamese currency) they had earned, and in many cases cheated from others. I slowly walked back to my villa, continually feeling the gaze of countless eyes. Here in Vietnam, Americans are never free of that look—that look tinted with the hope that you will purchase something, tinted with curiosity, tinted with fear, tinted with hate.

I went upstairs to our second story patio. The day was hazy. The clouds were covering the sun's offerings. My mood was one of relaxed amazement. The people down on the street were vigorously conducting their Saturday affairs. The bombs in the background had a chilling effect on this scene. I went and put Crosby, Stills, Nash & Young on the stereo. I opened the icebox and reached for a beer. Back on the patio I was again engulfed with the people on the street below. The record blares, "We can change the world, rearrange the world, it's dying, it's dying." A friend handed me a cigarette asking, "What does it mean?"

The afternoon sped by. Lazily it dawned on me that Saturday evening was almost at hand. What's on tap for tonight? Oh, probably the same things—hunt some "tuna" (girls), pretend that they care, pretend that it makes you happy. Suddenly I realized that I hadn't eaten yet. That's a good excuse to go to the hospital and get away from the villa for a while. I can go see my friend Randy. He was on call all night. Saturday night is always busy with emergency cases. For everyone's sake, I hoped tonight would be quiet.

The evening was dark and cloudy now. What appeared to be lightning lit up the sky in the background. Regrettably, I was aware that it wasn't lightning. After spending some time at the hospital, I decided to walk back to the villa. Maybe something was happening there. Walking on the narrow, muddy road to the villa, I became aware of a bar I had not seen before. I hesitated, then went in. Why not?

As I entered, I was blinded by the darkness. I could not even make out the face of the young Vietnamese girl who was hustling me off to a secluded corner. Slowly I regained my vision. I could see the girl who was now snuggled up to me. She was a few years younger, with the open look of approachable innocence. Her hair was soft, dark, and long. She wore a black and white mini-dress that did very little to cover her large rounded breasts. Her bare thighs came out from under the small dress. Her huge eyes seemed to be hypnotizing me. She was by far the most beautiful girl, by far the most desirable girl in the room. Her name was My Le.

"You got girlfriend?" she muttered, hoping that the answer would be no.

"No," I reassured her.

"When you leave Vietnam?" she inquired. I held up two hands to indicate ten months. This pleased her. By now the two drinks had come.

"Where you work?" she again wanted to know. This I also told her. She was so unbelievably beautiful. She looked up and touched my face, my nose, my mouth.

"You stay with me tonight?" she wanted to know. "You be my boyfriend. I number one girl."

The tempo increased as My Le intensified her caresses, her affection. Two more drinks came. By now I was aware that these were extra-strong gin and tonics. She ran her fingers through my hair.

"You have long hair, not like lifer."

"Yes, you see I'm not a typical solider. I was in school when I got drafted—law school. I had long hair then and don't at all believe in our involvement here." I suddenly looked up, aware that I wasn't back in America talking to a date. "You don't give a shit, do you," I stormed.

She looked at me with those huge, beautiful eyes. "You stay with me; you be my boyfriend," she reiterated. Two more drinks arrived.

"I have to go to a party," I said, making an excuse.

"When you come see me again?" she wanted to know.

I got up to leave, astonished at these Vietnamese. Hollywood has nothing on these people. These people act their lives out—that's how they survive. Indeed, we taught them well.

"You come tomorrow?" she persisted.

"Yes, I come tomorrow," I reassured her. Alone. I walked out into the rain, knowing I would never return.

Many hours later, after curfew, another tech and I dodged MPs up and down Saigon alleys. Those words spoken earlier by my friend at the villa came back to me.

"What does it mean?"

"Vietnam: What a tragic waste of life, love, and young laughter."
—George McGovern

THE WAR
Richard Pena, Fall 1972

"It was the best of times, it was the worst of times . . . in short, the period was so far like the present period, that some of its nosiest authorities insisted on its being received, for good or evil, in the superlative degree of comparison only."
— Charles Dickens, *A Tale of Two Cities*

IT IS WITHIN THIS WORLD THAT WE EXIST. IN THIS WAR SITUATION, IT IS AS if someone has stolen all sense of moderation; it is as if no middle range exists for events, beliefs, and emotions. For 365 days we are destined to live in this world of continuous extremes. War surely brings out the worst in people; it brings out the best in people. So many events happen which are worthy of note; however, each is soon surpassed in intensity by another event. "Why write anything at all?" I occasionally ask myself. Knowing the answer, I continue. There is a story here which must be told to all; there is a story here which must never be forgotten.

There are many different wars in Vietnam. We in 3rd Field Hospital see an entirely different war than is seen in Can-Tho, in the Delta. For this reason, only those of us who work together, who play together, who laugh together, who cry together in these days of intensity will understand the apparent contradiction of which I speak. This is the contradiction of extreme bitterness entwined with extreme tenderness.

It is difficult to describe these days in Vietnam when all one has are his friends. Exiled to a land halfway around the globe, the individuals of the OR have developed an unparalleled relationship. To say that we are close is to speak in an inferior realm. It is as if destiny has deliberately placed us together in this perilous time. The idealism of youth is all around, yet the wisdom of maturity prevails. In short, the members of the OR are as one. We have very little in Vietnam, yet we have ourselves.

The group is perhaps thirteen, perhaps fifteen. Numbers don't matter. Yet in a few short months we have built a companionship and trust that few people experience in a lifetime. Perhaps the reason is that we are confronted with death every day. Perhaps we attempt to offset the horrors and loneliness of war with friendship and acceptance. In this period of uncertain reality, our emotions swing to the extreme. Yes, we would gladly risk our lives for one another. My God, how young we are—how old we are!

That Thursday in August began as any other. Somewhere in this country Randy and I had planned to find a semblance of happiness. Of course, we were aware that it would only be artificial, for there is no true happiness for Americans in Vietnam.

"Ready for another?" I asked Randy as we downed our third round for the afternoon.

"Dickie, have you heard?" yelled Bill as he came in the door. "Mike and Rev are on the new drop list."

Which meant that they would be going home. Instantly, we were all enthusiastic. This was a dream come true for whoever was fortunate enough to make it through V.N. and go back to The World.

I don't remember much of what happened after that. Suddenly, we were all surrounding Mike in Vic's apartment. The news was broken to him. I thought he was going to soar through the roof.

"I've made it, I've made it," he screamed. I felt so happy for him, yet . . .

Later we told Rev. He cried.

It was not until the next day that we learned of the other OR techs who would also be leaving. I greeted this news with mixed emotions. Of course, they were ecstatic with joy.

"I want to go, yet I don't," Bruce would later relate. "I don't want to leave the rest of you here."

"One thing, Bruce," I asked. "Don't let them forget us."

The things that go through a person's mind on the eve of departure are strange. Each individual reacts in a different way. Yet there is a common denominator of thought which prevails. In those last few hours, those leaving speak of many things. Most, of course, are in that state of ecstatic happiness which is reached by an individual but a few times within a lifetime. This is a state in which the object of happiness is happiness itself and the event that triggers the happiness is but the vehicle. The balancing reaction to the many months of contempt and bitterness is finally emerging.

Yet theirs is not a total happiness, because they are leaving the rest of us behind. They are happy for themselves, but are worried about us. Of course we, the non-departers, share their joy with the acceptance of a reluctant lover being left behind. Although we will no longer have their companionship to ease the horror of this "theater of the absurd," a part of us will go with them. However, a much greater part of them will remain here with us.

How often, in the last seventy-two hours, they speak of a persistent concern and fear for those of us who will remain behind. We, of course, all promise to write. We, the non-departers, agree to send them that single precious commodity. In all, I am very glad to see them leave. I will no longer have to worry about them making it home alive. I reflect upon my self-proclaimed goal of being the last of my friends, of all Americans, to leave this country. I am determined to have my departure mark the end of this tragic era in American history.

In these last few hours we all realize the improbability of ever seeing each other again. However, we know that in future days each of us will reflect back to this time, to this place, and again we will touch. Of the many people in the world, only this small handful can ever understand what each of us experiences in this, the most difficult year of our lives.

Throughout these last seventy-two hours, the words keep crossing my mind: "We are, all of us, molded and remolded by those who have loved us; no love, no friendship, can ever cross the path of our destiny without leaving some mark upon it forever."

That Saturday evening was to be the night of the final farewell party. Mentally, everyone was looking forward to it as the time for goodbyes. We've all left people and places without even being aware that we were leaving. For some reason, an emptiness is felt inside if we leave in this manner—without a final goodbye.

The day had gone by rather quickly. Randy and I were on duty and were finishing things up, when a nurse from the ER came rushing in. Just from looking at her you could tell that something was happening. She radiated a sense of urgency.

"A C-130 just went down around Can-To," she said before we even had a chance to say hello. The ramifications of this raced through my mind.

"Any survivors?" Randy quickly asked.

"It's too early to tell," she said. "The first reports are that they might bring fourteen of them here."

There goes our party, I thought. Of all the nights to have mass causalities. Almost as an afterthought I asked, "How did it happen? Was it shot down?"

"Mechanical failure," she replied.

Typical Army.

The next few hours were given to preparation. Most of our back-up supplies were sterilized. Burn dressing and linen packs were made up. Anyone who dropped by the OR began helping. Soon everyone who worked in the OR had heard of the emergency and had come by to see if we needed assistance. Usually in these life-or-death emergencies, the compassion of people comes through very vividly. What the hell, we had long ago ceased functioning as separate entities. We were all in this together.

The dread could be seen in everyone's eyes. Glances purposefully did not meet. Perhaps it was because we knew what was to come. We all had seen burn patients before. They are the worst kind to take mentally. I hate them because they bring home the horrors of this senseless war. Burns are a very special type of wound, and no one likes caring for them. Serious burns are very difficult to look at, and too often the patients die.

Within a few hours the patients started coming in. We discovered that only four had survived. One of those was burned too badly to be taken into surgery immediately. He died shortly after arriving at the hospital. The first of the patients was rolled into the OR. To an outsider, it might have appeared that everyone was running about in a confused manner. However, everyone has a function in the OR, and what may seem to be mass confusion is actually the most expedient way of saving lives.

I was surprised to see the Chaplain in the OR. Were the survivors that bad? A glance at the first soldier answered my question. The skin on his face appeared to be plastered red. His hair and eyebrows had been burned away. The red burns ran the length of the young soldier's body. He was so young.

There is not much that can be done for burns. Sulfamylon cream was smeared all over his burned body. You feel so helpless. There's not a damn thing you can do. We all silently added up his percentage for life, as if he would have any type of life if he did survive. I checked his chart. He had a wife and young child.

As I was leaving the operating room, Bob stopped me.

"How's it going in there?" he inquired.

I looked up. "He's going to die."

We do not get a distorted picture of the patients in Vietnam. They come to us as soon as they have been injured. We see kids burned, kids full of holes, kids dying. They have not been treated elsewhere; they come to us right from the battlefield.

Soon the next patient was rolled into the OR. This one was not very bad off, comparatively speaking. He had a broken ankle and numerous lacerations. He was a sergeant. For some reason I feel less infuriated when professional soldiers come into the OR. They know the risk involved when they choose their career. The ones that we see in the OR are simply the ones that lose at the game. The kids though—they are the ones that really get you. Most have been drafted and put here at someone else's whim. The lifers can control their destiny; the draftees cannot.

I never cease to wonder how a president can play God and politics with the lives of people. How many dead will it take for them to see?

The patient was under a local anesthetic. We couldn't give him a general because he had a broken nose. While the surgeon repaired his ankle, I was prepping a laceration close to his face. Suddenly the sergeant looked at me. He was very drowsy.

"Doc, doc," he said to me, almost in a prayer. "I want to thank you for what you are doing."

I knew what he was thinking. He thought I was a doctor and had helped save his life. Somehow I could not bear to tell him that I wasn't the doctor. The next instant my mind was flashing to the Buck Slip (medical sheet). It would read "non-combat wound." I looked at him again. It was all there in his eyes. The pain, the helplessness, the fear and the questions he'd never asked about this war.

"Sarge, you'll be all right. You were very lucky," was all I could respond with. I could not tell him that he was not receiving anything special. I could not tell him that he was considered nothing more than another patient, that his name was even misspelled on the Buck Slip. This war, this suffering, and the atrocities committed against mankind had made us all callous to some degree. You try your best to prevent it, but there is so much suffering that this callous barrier is perhaps a defense mechanism. It helps you keep your sanity in Vietnam.

It was incredible how lucky this sergeant was. He was banged up pretty bad, but there would be no permanent injury. He called to me again.

"How are the rest of the fellas? There were some really fine boys on that plane. Did you bring a Watson in here? He'd just gotten into the country. How about an Evans?"

"We have no word on many of the passengers," I responded. This was not the time to tell him that only three had survived.

"How many were in the plane?" I asked him.

"Forty, maybe forty-five."

That was considerably greater than the figure of fourteen released by government sources. But things like that are expected in Vietnam. Even the lowest soldier feels insulted by the figures put out about this war. We always have a larger kill factor than the other side. Always.

But then being misinformed, being brainwashed is expected in Vietnam. Things are expected here. People are expected to get burned, others to have legs blown off, some to be blinded; people are expected to be killed. These things are expected, but this is a hard explanation for the victims to live with. These mangled human beings will not return to American society as they left, with the only justification for their individual nightmares being that it is expected.

We finished up late in the OR that night. The party that was once so important seemed to have passed ages ago. It was so inconsequential now, although it had been a gallant attempt to forget the realities of our situation. Tomorrow they would be on that "Freedom Bird," going home. The next day a new bunch would arrive. This insane cycle would begin again. You cannot predict whether a certain individual will live to see his home again. The only thing you can safely say is that once a person comes to Vietnam, he will never be the same again.

"America, I have paid my dues. Leave me to my misery."
—Anonymous Vietnam Participant

CAST OF PARTICIPANTS
Richard Pena, Fall 1972

RICH SICARD: RICH WAS FROM MASS. HE HAD GOTTEN BUSTED FOR GRASS and was in the Army as an alternative to jail. He was the greatest lover in the bunch. He had been in Vietnam longer than me, and it was from him that I learned how to deal with the Vietnamese people.

Brother Leary: Luther was a number-one stud in the true sense of the word. He was outstandingly smooth and fluent with his rap. We spent many hours discussing ideas and The World. We learned from each other. The spark of revolution was rekindled within him.

Randy Borzilleri (Bozo): My closest friend in Vietnam. We offset each other in many ways. Our goal was to help each other maintain a semblance of sanity in this place. His father was an orthopedic surgeon. His family founded a hospital in Buffalo. He, too, wanted to be a surgeon, but we shared the knowledge that he probably would not be accepted to medical school. He was excellent in the operating room. He rushed home on the day of the presidential election. His mother was dying of cancer. His Vietnam experience had taught him how to deal with and accept death.

Bill Blackwell: He was from Virginia and had one of the best heads around. We both shared the same bitterness. He had great potential. We were friends.

Dawg: Another Southerner, Dawg was from Georgia. A good friend. He wrote us when he got back to The World. "It don't mean shit." He was referring to a saying we use in Vietnam. The "It" can be anything the Vietnam solider wants it to be. To many of us "It" symbolizes anything that is bad.

Mike Aguilar: Still involved in the social world of the post-high school era. Through his constant activity he helped everyone maintain their sanity. We were close associates. He wrote back that The World no longer cared about Vietnam.

Bruce Edberg: Bruce was a compassionate, considerate person. All he wanted was to get back to his wife.

Vic Ponce: Vic was of the same breed as Bruce, gentle and considerate. He almost fell in love with a Vietnamese girl.

John Buydos: John possessed a good head. A gentle, good person. Like us all, he wanted only to get out of Vietnam. We were together until the very end.

Jody French: He had completed his third year of medical school at McGill when he got drafted. His family possessed upper-class wealth, yet here he was no different from anyone else. Part of the Woodstock generation. We shared a mutual respect.

John Goodwin: Claimed to have an ecstatically happy marriage. He came from a difficult background. He tried very hard to be liked. He was a friend. He helped us survive.

Larry Paulsen: Another draftee sent to Vietnam. He had no respect for Army bullshit, nor did he comply with it. This quality attracted me to him. New avenues of growth were opened for him in Vietnam. He expanded himself a great deal here. He became radicalized.

Rev: Young. He was in love and wanted to marry his high school sweetheart. Friends wrote that she was not waiting around for him.

Sau Yung: Brilliant. Med school was his goal. He and I were the last OR personnel to leave Vietnam.

Larry McCalley: A good person with a sense of humor. He wanted to get back to his wife and to teaching. He wanted to get back to sanity.

Ken Bailey: A quiet, thoughtful tech. He attempted to insulate himself from the war more than others. I hope he succeeded.

George: George was on his third tour of Vietnam. He had married a Vietnamese woman, and they had a daughter. After his last two tours, she had promised to meet him in America but never came. On this tour she was to make it three for three.

There were of course many more actors in this American tragedy. However, the above were the most memorable to me.

R AND R
Richard Pena, Fall 1972

AFTER SIX MONTHS IN VIETNAM, I TAKE R & R IN HAWAII. AS MY PLANE touches down in Honolulu, I know that I am about to re-enter a world in which I have long ago ceased to live. Yet, I am not prepared for my initial reaction to the people of the American culture. For the first time in my life, I view America as an outsider might. Everything seems so strange. I feel alien, almost as a "stranger in a strange land."

I wonder if I will ever again assimilate into this society. I wonder if I really want to. The period and the degree of assimilation when one returns to America is different for each individual. Indeed, many, even those who return physically intact, may never readapt. My initial feeling of displacement was followed by a period of depression and bitterness, then by the realization that I've forgotten how to laugh. The heavy burden has not been lifted, for I realize that I must go back to that place. I cannot forget the people who remain there. It seems so distant, while sitting amidst the luxuries of civilization—almost as a dream.

They, the American people, view me as an oddity and with suspicion. (1) I am a serviceman, and (2) I have been in Vietnam. Yet, I can be nothing but repulsed at the manner in which they carry on—the materialism, the self-centeredness, the rudeness. Above all, I am struck by their ignorance and disinterest in the disastrous foreign policy our country is engaged in. The six months I have spent in Vietnam seem an eternity. I have seen so many horrors in that time.

When a soldier re-enters The World from Nam, he views things from an entirely different perspective than ever before. I, for one, find myself being very impatient with the American people who I feel have sent me to Vietnam by virtue of their apathy and loss of interest in the war. The checks and balances of our system are designed to make Congress responsive to the will of the people. But, in this case, the negative feedback by the population simply has not been sufficient.

Now, as I return to The World, even for a brief period, I feel the people really don't care what happens to me—just as they don't care about the innocent people getting killed in Southeast Asia. That is, not until their sons and daughters get drafted and start dying. By then, the wheels have already been set in motion and it is too late.

They, the American public, the ones that have been silent, have sat idly by as more than 55,000 Americans have been killed in vain, more than 500,000 wounded, and countless others have been permanently impaired. When the facts are told to these silent people, they do not scream at the horror that their silence has caused; instead, they turn the channel. Don't they care that 2.5 million Americans have been made to suffer the abominations of this insane war because of a miscalculation by a few political leaders? This is not a necessary war; rather, it is a blunder. Don't they care about the mutilated and burned, about the legs and arms and eyes that are being lost? Or don't they care enough to find out?

My friends in The World tell me not to be so hard on these Americans that are silent. Ask those who have been made to suffer through this hell of a war, ask the 55,000 dead, the maimed, their wives and their mothers whether their silence deserves to be forgiven.

PART III

IN THE HOSPITAL
John Hagan

ALTHOUGH THE 3RD FIELD HOSPITAL WHERE RICHARD SERVED IN SAIGON was not a Mobile Army Surgical Hospital like the kind portrayed in MASH, there were strong parallels, mostly demonstrated through the black humor used for tension relief in both circumstances. The U.S. Army called it a field hospital, but the 3rd was really a full-fledged medical facility with state-of-the-art equipment and specialists. While the 3rd traced its lineage to Korea and World War II, the Army reconstituted the unit in 1965 by deploying personnel from Fort Lewis, Washington.

The hospital, formerly the American Community School in Saigon prior to the war, was the in-country destination for wounded American soldiers who needed sophisticated emergency medical care. Although it started with only 100 beds, the hospital grew into nine separate wards. The facility treated medical issues ranging from urological reconstructive surgery to opium withdrawal and heroin addiction.

The reconfigured hospital contained elevated beds commandeered from the Vietnam Army Medical Depot, typewriters requisitioned from the American embassy, and desks and bookcases taken

73

from a former school. The nurses wore uniforms called "whites," a rarity in Vietnam. As a veteran of service in the 3rd Field Hospital recalled:

> Working twelve-hour shifts and sometimes around the clock at 3rd Field was no picnic. . . . We had a kidney dialysis unit to deal with traumatically wounded [soldiers] in renal failure, [which] meant we cared for the most seriously wounded in Vietnam. I remember periods when doctors and nurses rarely left the hospital, and after a twelve-hour shift in the Renal Unit, I and many others helped in the Triage area when the flow was heavy.[20]

The 3rd Field Hospital in Saigon was where the patients from MASH units all over Vietnam wound up. The outlying MASH units saw the worst cases first before airlifting them to the 3rd. The G.I. John Ketwig describes the arrival by helicopter of a group of injured soldiers into Saigon:

> "The chopper settled onto the steel plating, its rotor blades driving the gray water in hammering sheets that made the steel walls resound. A door slid open horizontally, and the medics ran forward into the wash. A dark, broken hulk of a man lowered himself to the metal floor, hunched below the whirling blades, and dragged a wounded leg toward me. A second form loomed out of the mist, his arm bandaged and misshapen. A third, naked to the waist, with an olive-drab field dressing held to his ear, blood washing over heavily muscled shoulders to a hairy chest. The medics, some women, frantically worked at a stretcher, lifting it to a gurney and rushing toward sanctuary from the stinging rain. Another broke out of the mist at the front of the chopper. A final dark figure came out of the wash,

holding a wadded fatigue shirt to his side, his torso a dark brown.

"I stepped back as the distorted troupe moved nearer, as the stretchers bumped and wobbled toward the overhead door. It was chaotic, messy. The door slid down, muffling some of the clatter of the rain and the ascending chopper. A new sound rose in the metal room, banging off the walls, pitiful in its painful, morphine-clouded misery. 'My leg! My God my leg! What am I gonna tell my wife? Oh, it hurts. I can't feel my foot, my knee hurts so bad! My God! My God! Help me!' He was young, but big and muscular. A red trail ran off the stretcher to the floor, to mix with the water there. Two soaking medics—one male, one female—attacked the leg, cutting the shredded wet fabric, tying off the stump of the leg. It was gone below the knee, a gory stump of red-and-pink meat. The soldier screamed with more terror than pain. . . . The morphine was slurring the screams as they wheeled the stretcher deeper into the building."[21]

These injured and dying American soldiers received high-quality emergency treatment from American medics—a standard of care that was only rarely available to the massive number of injured Vietnamese soldiers and civilians.

In 1971, the Vietnam Veterans Against the War gathered in Detroit to hold the Winter Soldier Investigations, which documented the nature of medical care in the Vietnam War. Jon Bjornson, a medic who had resigned his commission after serving in 1964 and 1965 with the 8th Field Hospital in Nha Trang, convened a medical panel and served as a moderator for the hearings. Bjornson's testimony included descriptions of the triage system used to sort the injured: "Americans got the best [care]. If an ARVN [South Vietnamese soldier] had the same type of problem, . . . he got the second best. Prisoners got the worst by far."

Twenty-year-old David Fortin from the Third Marine Division described the torture of prisoners in military hospitals:

> "They'd come down with ITT, which is Intelligence Translations people, and they try to get information from the prisoners. If the prisoner wouldn't give information out to the questions they asked, they'd use various ways of torture. They'd poke at his wounds. I've seen them stand a prisoner up who had a stomach wound; his shoulder was torn up. They generally harassed the prisoner until they could get information out of him."

David Galicia was a psychiatrist who served at Saigon's 3rd Field Hospital a year or two before Richard Pena arrived. He testified that the Vietnamese civilians were keenly aware of the difference in quality of care at the American 3rd and Saigon's own Choi Rhe hospital. The 3rd's emergency room personnel treated ordinary Vietnamese civilians using the U.S. military's triage system:

> "When [Vietnamese civilians] came in, they were actually refused treatment in the emergency room. They might get a cursory going over if they were brought in by our ambulance in the triage areas. The standing order was that if he was in such rough shape that he might die any moment, you just stuck a bottle of D5W, glucose water, in his arm. You use a plasmic expander or something so that they can be taken to the ARVN hospitals."

Galicia went on to describe the subpar conditions at Choi Rhe hospital. Beds were shared by up to three people in rooms that were infested with cockroaches. Because the hospital had few trained staff, family members ended up caring for the patients. Even when space was available, Galicia reported, the 3rd turned away Vietnamese—

unless they were high-ranking officials:

"We took care of the Prime Minister, his family, and anybody who had a position or any authority within the Vietnamese government. . . . You'd know they were there because there were a dozen cars, there were all kinds of personnel to protect these people, and we actively treated these people."

Galicia described the official hierarchy of the 3rd Field Hospital and the unofficial ways in which he and others sometimes circumvented its rules. His description of the ranking medical officer was right out of *MASH*: "He was a fully qualified internist, but he never practiced a day of medicine when I was there. His rounds consisted of glad-handing all the VIPs that happened to be in the hospital at any one particular time."

Like Richard Pena, Galicia found that the familial atmosphere amongst the Americans at the 3rd Field Hospital did not extend to the Vietnamese civilians who worked there:

> "Within the family of the hospital, itself, I remember one occasion in which I overheard one of my techs talking to a girl who worked within the hospital, hospital cleaning. . I learned that this girl's brother was ill. She lived out in the alley, and, after all, she did work for us; this kind of made her part of the family. . . . I went with this girl later on to the family's home, and I determined that this was a five-year-old boy who had pneumonia. I went back and I asked if he could be brought in. I was flat out told no. I then asked if I could have the medication to go out and treat him, and I was again told no. So I stole the penicillin and went and treated him anyway."

It was a fact that most of the thousands of permanently injured civilians on the streets of Saigon were victims of what the Vietnamese called the American War. Many had amputated limbs from exploded bombs and mines. Even more disturbing were the wounds caused by U.S.-sourced napalm and white phosphorous. Galicia saw the effects of napalm on workers around the hospital:

> One I distinctly remember was a lady I used to see out in the yard in between two of the wards. This lady had been burned beyond recognition, facial-wise. She had no face. Her eyes were left, and they had somehow or another grafted some skin over the front of her head. She had some sort of orifice left that she could take food through, but that's about it. She'd been the victim of napalm.

White phosphorus was no less devastating in Vietnam. Galicia learned firsthand at the 3rd that "white phosphorous is not something that if it hits you, you can put out. You have to carve it out, because it'll burn its way through anything, especially if you're speaking in terms of humans. It burns through anything—flesh, bones—till it gets to the other side and falls out."

Napalm and white phosphorous were not the only substances that wreaked havoc in Vietnam. Drug use and partying happened after hours at the villa and in clubs and bars around Saigon. Cheap subsidized beer—"This one's for you"—was the military's answer to the easily accessible and highly addictive pharmacopeia of the Vietnam War. Snapshots of Richard and his friends at the villa reveal an abundance of beer and marijuana, as well as attractive young women. The local police raided the villa one night and searched the rooms at gunpoint for the women. To the intense frustration of the police, the women successfully hid themselves behind a false wall in an upstairs room.

The Vietnam War created plenty of alcoholics and drug addicts. The 3rd Field Hospital even had an entire floor devoted to American soldiers with drug addictions. Despite this, the military never acknowledged the extent of the problem and had no effective policy for providing meaningful treatment. Galicia illustrated the problem by describing "a black kid who came in on six different occasions. He had shot up 30 cc of heroin or opium a day, 4 cc at a crack—seven or eight times a day."

Still, the U.S. Army had no procedure for sending addicted soldiers out of the country for treatment, and narcotic drugs were so readily available in Vietnam that they were difficult to avoid. "Just about any kind of drug that you can think of, from heroin on down, if you couldn't get it from one of the guys in the hospital, it could be bought downtown," Galicia said. "It was no problem to get drugs up on the ward, even."

Lacking the methods or resources to treat them, the 3rd Field Hospital sent most of the addicted soldiers back to their units. Galicia explained that a soldier "would be taken by the MPs back to some MP unit, then be released to his company commander again because there [was] such a rampant problem they didn't have the space for these people. They didn't know what the fuck to do with them, so they ended up giving them back to the company commander. The company commander . . . put the man back to work, and, of course, this man would be back in the hospital again."

Galicia tried to find an unofficial solution, as he had with the child who had pneumonia:

> I harbored a few of these people for a while. Most of my patients were on Ward 8. I would sneak these people up to Ward 9, which was a convalescent ward, and again I got bombarded from the hospital itself, because regulations there said I couldn't keep anybody for more than thirty days—I got called down front many times, accused of harboring individuals, and I confessed to it, but these were people who had been in so many times, you know, it was like clockwork. Three days or four days from the time I let them out, they'd be back.

The approach of the 3rd Field Hospital mirrored policies used throughout the armed forces to wean soldiers off drugs: they found temporary solutions but never tried to address the underlying addictions.

As individual soldiers searched for a way to escape from the war and the sense of collective defeat, the rise of alcoholism and drug addiction became both symbolic and symptomatic of the U.S. military failure. Drug addiction became an ominous metaphor for the war itself as American and South Vietnamese morale crumbled. The sociological term for this feeling of malaise is "anomie," taken from the French word for normlessness or purposelessness. "Who would be the last American and Vietnamese to die for this mistake?" John Kerry had asked. As the unwinnable war continued, battle after battle, his question reverberated as if in an echo chamber.

Still, it would be several more months before Sau and Richard climbed aboard the last planes, filled with the final combat troops, to leave Vietnam.

The operating room is filled with so much tragedy.
Those who are exposed to this suffering instinctively surround
themselves with a callousness quite unlike their normal character.

THIS WAR'S FOR REAL
Richard Pena, Fall 1972

AN ALLIED CAMBODIAN WAS FLOWN TO THE HOSPITAL ON A SATURDAY IN September. He had been shot by a mini-gun from one of our Cobras. Evidently, another case of mistaken identity. This war produces quite a few such incidents.

As it was a Saturday, few people were at the hospital. I was present because I was on call. The lab summoned me to give some blood for the Cambodian. I was the only person available on this particular day with B positive blood. Immediately after I had given the blood, I was informed that he was coming into the OR. It was a desperate attempt to save his life. The doctors stated that he couldn't survive an operation, yet he wouldn't survive without one. What a war!

Not only did I have to give my blood, but minutes later I was assisting in the operation. The Cambodian had his left leg amputated. I stared at my own blood as it splattered all over the OR floor.

My mind flashed to what my friends in Austin would be doing at that very instant. The Texas Longhorns were opening the 1972 football season that night. My friends were probably sitting in the stands between the twenty and forty-yard lines—all would have dates. It suddenly struck me that they were immune to the realities and horrors of war. Watching a football game seemed so trivial in comparison to the loss of life. How I envied them.

We had other cases that night. When I finally got off work the following morning I slept for twenty-six of the next thirty hours. The Cambodian died the next day.

*   *   *

Rich and I came to work shortly after dawn this Sunday. Our early morning routine was interrupted as soon as we saw the activity in the ER. Curiosity overtook us both, and we walked over to check out what was going on. We stood a few feet away from a litter with a white disposable sheet pulled over the corpse. It was not unusual to have someone die in the emergency room, but every death made us angry.

This nineteen-year-old American soldier died from a gunshot wound to the head. He was walking the streets of Pleiku the previous night when another American asked him for a cigarette. He replied that he did not have one and kept on walking. The American who had asked pulled out a .38 pistol and shot the nineteen-year-old in the back of the head at point-blank range. His bodily functions had ceased at 6:00 a.m. that Sunday morning. It is shameless how death toys with one's life in Vietnam, how it makes fun of our most precious possession. A feeling of impermanence swept over me. All my previous concerns seemed so small and unimportant.

*   *   *

A young American soldier was on the operating table. A team of doctors in the emergency room had diagnosed this as a neuro case. The surgeon drilled burr holes in an attempt to save the patient's life. The operating team did not know why, but the young soldier was rapidly dying.

The surgeon rushed through the operation because his main concern was not to have the patient die on the operating table—it's simply bad business. There are so many forms to fill out, so many implications, etc. Hurriedly, he was taken off the table and wheeled into intensive care to die. It was discovered there that the soldier had a stomach wound and had died from internal bleeding. Mistake?

Misdiagnosis? Win a few, lose a few? Call it what you will. It is all part of this absurd war.

* * *

Bravery, stupidity, incompetence, fear, love, humanitarianism. All are accented and take on a greater meaning in a war situation because each of these traits has an impact on human life.

* * *

In mid-June an Army captain's leg was amputated. Those who still possessed a sense of humanity were furious. The amputation was necessary because the American surgeon who did the initial leg surgery negligently tied a vein to an artery and an artery to a vein.

* * *

In late June the orthopedic surgeons had to sneak a young Vietnamese girl into the hospital because we were not authorized to treat Vietnamese civilians. However, the girl's legs would take extensive work to save, and the American surgeons knew that her legs would almost certainly be amputated if they were to send her to the Vietnamese hospital. Amputation was the regular "cure-all" at the Vietnamese hospital because it was much faster and easier than corrective surgery.

The American doctors did extensive surgery on the young girl without the hospital commander's permission and under threat of severe reprimand.

* * *

Christmas in Vietnam:

It was early December. In America, people were preparing for the Christmas season. However, in Vietnam things were entirely different. The days were still very hot and dangerous. The nights, likewise. The Peace Talks were again deadlocked. There was little cause for optimism. I had never before spent Christmas in a foreign land. Curious, I asked a veteran soldier who had spent last Christmas in Nam what it was like. "There is no Christmas in Vietnam," he said, "and Easter is a big finger."

I posed the same question to a Vietnamese girl. She replied, "No, there is not a Christmas in Vietnam. There is not too much to be thankful for here." Then, as an afterthought she laughingly said, "Besides, Santa Claus is afraid to come to Vietnam because he'll get shot down."

Later that month I found out how very right they were. War knows no holidays.

* * *

I spent the day after Christmas doing a craniotomy on a twenty-year-old American soldier named John. He and a companion had gotten drunk on Christmas day and gone for a joyride in a jeep, which they drunkenly rammed into the back of a large military truck. John's friend was DOA (dead on arrival), and John was permanently blinded before he got into the OR.

We were in surgery for more than four hours trying to save him. The surgeon succeeded, but because his condition included severe brain damage, I wondered what type of life he would have. It was listed in the weekly casualty reports as a Non-Combat Wound. No one on the OR team blamed John for his reckless action. He was merely trying to forget where he was, trying to find a bit of joy in the hell he'd been put in. The Army will, of course, tell his parents that the military, Vietnam, and the President's madness were not responsible for their son's unfortunate accident.

* * *

The agony of Vietnam is painfully palpable in each individual. Our one common aim is to get the hell out of Vietnam. Some find a way to ride out the nightmare. Others devise ways to get out prematurely. Steve is one such person. He loaded a mortar round, held his hand over the exit opening and fired. He got out of Vietnam all right, but he blew his hand off in the process.

*   *   *

One young soldier who was in surgery for fourteen hours would perhaps have considered Steve's decision wise. He was sent home a tri-amputee. His right leg was disarticulated at the hip. Left leg amputated above the knee. Right arm amputated at the shoulder. Three fingers of the remaining hand were removed. Part of the stomach was taken out. Part of the kidney. He lost his right eye plus nine feet of intestine. The right side of his face consisted of a skin flap. The face of war.

"If the United States is saving the people of South Vietnam from communism, who will save them from Americanism?"
—Anonymous Vietnam Participant

THE PEOPLE
Richard Pena, Winter 1972

THE WAR IN VIETNAM, LIKE MANY OTHER WARS, IS FILTHY, AGONIZING, degrading, and senseless. Americans long ago recognized that their involvement in this war was a diplomatic catastrophe and a military disaster at best. Yet the spectrum of horrors perpetrated in Vietnam goes beyond the visible American failures. Whatever the reason—memories of manifest destiny, American ethnocentrism, Pax Americana, or simply American values—the welfare of the people we are fighting to save has somehow been forgotten.

It strikes me as curious that in this so called democratic regime of Vietnam the people are not being asked for their opinion, nor is their best interest being considered. For whose best interest, then, are we fighting?

This question has perplexed most American soldiers who have been in Vietnam. Perhaps the answer lies in the words spoken by a marine sergeant when he said, "There are two types of gooks: the ones fighting on the other side—who really work—and the ones fighting for us."

It seems interesting to me that he discounted the theory that we were fighting for them. But in this war, everything is turned upside down. We dehumanize the Vietnamese. We call them names and look for the worst in them, never trying to understand what they are going through. One soldier told me, "It's war, damn it. We are here to kill them; they are here to kill us. It's war, damn it."

In reality, it is the Vietnamese people who have suffered the most from this conflict. Yet it is their wants and needs which receive the least attention. The government of South Vietnam in 1972 is nothing short of a totalitarian dictatorship. President Thieu has declared martial law, eliminating all elections and freedom of speech. The newspapers are censored. Only a few, which are sympathetic to the government, are allowed to exist.

In 1972 the war is still going on and the people are still suffering. Saigon has close to three million inhabitants—many of them piaster worshipers. There are, of course, many different types of Vietnamese in Saigon. It would be tremendously inaccurate to say that all can be put in the same category. There are, however, certain traits, which I find to be common to an overwhelming majority of the inhabitants.

Vietnamese society is not like ours. They have different priorities, different values, different morals. They, very simply, are products of their underdeveloped country. As such, they do not possess the sophistication of Americans, nor the idealism of American youth. To say that they are prisoners of the piaster is somewhat superficial, for they in fact dedicate their entire efforts toward survival.

The Americans here look with indignation at the Vietnamese and their methods. Most Americans do not even attempt to understand the causes behind the Vietnamese behavior. Would we, as "civilized" Americans, not take on similar characteristics if our basic survival was uncertain from day to day?

The basic misunderstanding arises from the fact that America attempted to force policies laced with idealism on a country where mere existence is paramount and idealism unheard of. This one misunderstanding can be detected in every realm—from our policy of implementing capitalism and democracy in this country to the average G.I. who gets murdered because he would not give a cyclo driver an extra fifty piaster (twelve cents).

The war is very much fought here in Saigon. It is immediately at hand. Every day you can hear it, you can see it. Yet the people continue about their business of survival, as if oblivious to the bombings in the background, to the flashes in the sky, to the planes, and to the flares at night.

War is a unique and temporary experience to the Americans in Vietnam; to the Vietnamese it is an assumed way of life. They pay little or no attention to the commonplace indicators of war. Nor do they let the horrors of war distract from their everyday lives. However, it is incorrect to say that the Vietnamese are an inhumane people. To them, war may be perfectly natural and as such so are its byproducts.

Saigon represents many things to many people. My views and impressions might be different but for this war. But it is in these times that a number of us exist and experience Saigon. Sometimes, looking for a good time, we go into dubious bars where we get mobbed by girls the moment we enter. Other times we simply ride around Saigon in a cyclo late at night or go into certain parlors. Of course, terrorists are ever-present, and by election time Americans have become prime targets. However, we are quick to conform to the existential world we are thrown into.

We never make plans beyond the day. The simple fact is that things change drastically from day to day. Our fellow Americans, friends that we work with, get killed unpredictably. The danger comes from every direction and in every form. In late 1972, the American war casualties are at a low. That, however, is not to say that Americans are not dying in Vietnam. Many are being called non-combat deaths and therefore not counted in the combat death toll. These deaths occur as a result of Americans merely being in Vietnam. This type of death is commonplace. We live with danger twenty-four hours a day.

Another element, which enhances the absurdity, is that the enemy is not always recognizable. For example, two medics at the hospital went on a supply run to Long Binh. The deuce-and-a-half truck they were driving went off the road, killing both soldiers. The accident resulted from a faulty part. Those in charge continued to send others out in similar malfunctioning vehicles. At times, the enemy is within.

Brother Holley was a medic at the hospital. A clean-cut American, he was devoted to his wife and child. He never drank, never smoked, didn't play around, and even went to church. Those traits are rare ordinarily, but in Vietnam they are almost impossible to find. Brother Holley submitted to the bodily passions only once. He was found dead the next morning in a lover's embrace. The girl had put ground-up glass in his food. Brother Holley was the sixth American the girl had murdered.

The women of Vietnam are a story all to themselves. They are a mirror image of American women, but without the filter screen of sophistication. In Saigon, they are plentiful. Some appear to be old, if nothing else in knowledge; others seem so very young. Many are beautiful, especially those that are half-French, half-Vietnamese or Chinese. We are told that the women migrate to Saigon from all over the country, for this is where the G.I.s are, and thus the money. Surprisingly, they can all speak English.

In our villa, there is a steady stream of women. Some stay for a while, some don't. Most of them are looking for a relationship. Most of us are not. It's hard to tell what they are really looking for. It's usually not hard to tell what the American soldier is looking for. It's easy for a female in America to look down at the Vietnamese women in Saigon, but to these individuals I would ask, "What would you do in the same situation?" It's war.

Thousands of pages have been written about the Vietnamese people. Yet, even with vivid descriptions and accounts, it is virtually impossible for an American who has not been to Vietnam to comprehend what the people here are like. The Vietnamese are of an Eastern culture and so they sometimes view things differently than we of a Western culture.

No one can be prepared for this, but having taken some Eastern philosophy courses in college, I have more of a background than most of my friends here. What I am learning is that the actions and reactions of some of the people here sometimes have an entirely different meaning than the interpretation given by the Western mind. For example, they sometimes nod, smile and say "yes" when in fact they mean "no." The Vietnamese are reflective of Eastern cultures in that the beliefs of the Vietnamese people cannot be deduced solely from overt actions.

It is for this very reason that I ask Vietnamese, with whom I have carefully built a friendship, various questions. I have every reason to believe that the answers they give are candid and honest. This is not to say that the individual opinions reflect the attitudes of the entire Vietnamese society. However, after discussing several issues with many Vietnamese, a basic set of beliefs, hopes, and fears does emerge.

Transcribed below are interviews with female acquaintances of the soldiers that live in the villa or that work in the hospital. Males are not generally available as they are either in the military, do not speak English, do not view us as friends, or are trying to kill us. There is a bright, young Vietnamese male that regularly comes by the villa. We have taken a real liking to him. Unfortunately, he cannot speak, and perhaps that is why he is not in the military. He is known to us as "Speechless."

The following are actual accounts, which I find representative of the feelings of the Vietnamese I have come to know while stationed here.

* * *

Hoa is a South Vietnamese nurse who is being trained at our hospital. One day we were busy at work preparing supplies. It was right before the presidential election of 1972. We had been discussing various OR procedures for some time.

"What do you think of Vietnam?" I asked.

"I want country to be one, but think never happen. I do not know why war cannot stop." Then she stopped, still thinking. I thought that perhaps she was groping for the correct words. She continued, "When be election?"

I was taken by surprise. "In several days," I responded.

"Who you want win?" Hoa inquired.

"McGovern."

"You think he end war?" she asked.

"He'll get Americans out," I answered.

"You think he win?"

"No," I confessed.

"Very sorry," Hoa said as she looked up. Then she continued with her work.

I was very surprised by this reply because all previous Vietnamese I have talked with want Nixon to win. The reason is not difficult to grasp. Thieu has complete control of the news media and has proceeded to characterize McGovern as a lunatic and Nixon as a saint. Many Vietnamese, as well as the military, want American involvement to continue in Vietnam. I must admit that the Stars and Stripes is not much more objective than the Vietnamese press.

*   *   *

Twee was the girlfriend of one of my housemates. We were in his room discussing light topics. Then she started getting serious. "Before beaucoup (very many) G.I., now tee-tee (few). Before America give Vietnam beaucoup (very much) money. Take Vietnam oil, gold."

Christ, I thought. Even she knows.

*   *   *

Snow was one of the more articulate Vietnamese girls. The evening had been warm and clear. We had spent most of it on the roof but were now in my room.

"You like Thieu?" I asked her.

"He be number 10,000 (bad). Everyone know that." She seemed a little impatient.

"What about Diem?" I continued. "Do you know who killed him?"

"Some people say he not dead. I think maybe he still be alive. They say he live in hills. Come back someday."

I was somewhat surprised at this legend. How true it is that a martyr never dies. I pressed on. "You like Vietnam?"

"It be my country. Where I can go? I no like Thieu. I no like killing. I no like blood. But what I can do? Where I can go?"

The evening hours passed into the night. I would look at her and wanted so much to trust in her, but I had long ago learned to distrust all Vietnamese. It was war.

*   *   *

"You leave four more months?" Sung asked me.

"Yes, I think so," I replied honestly.

"I think so too." She continued. "When G.I. leave, V.C. come to Saigon. I go Cambodia, then maybe Thailand. One time beaucoup (many) V.C. at Long Binh. I beaucoup (very) scared. 1968, V.C. come. Friend me, girlfriend G.I. They kill her, tear her apart."

*   *   *

I have become accustomed to hearing about the inhumane acts committed by the Viet Cong. One girl told me of how they had entered into her home and killed her mother and father. She had escaped with her life only by running. Another had seen the breast of her sister cut off. The massacres and murders were many. As a result, the South Vietnamese people are terrified of the Viet Cong. There is no side of justice in this war. Atrocities upon atrocities are committed—by every side involved.

*   *   *

A girl I'd met at the hospital spoke to me of the Vietnamese reaction to mixed babies.

"French babies unwanted," she said. "French soldiers come into village. Think all men work for Ho Chi Minh. Be 1945, maybe 1946. They come into village, kill men, rape women. French babies not liked by Vietnamese. Vietnamese like American babies (half-American, half-Vietnamese) tee-tee (little) more, but they not accepted."

*   *   *

Kim gave me some insight into their customs and superstitious legends. I had observed many Vietnamese with black teeth. My curiosity was stirred.

Me: "Why do people have black teeth?" (I was told it was from chewing betel nut, a tobacco that brings a high.)

Kim: "They dye."

Me: "You mean they paint all their teeth black?"

Kim: "Yes. It be an old Vietnamese custom. Different people Vietnam paint different. Some people take out all but two teeth."

Me: "No shit."

Kim: "Yes. You know people in the mountains—they have tail. It be little tail. My father bring one home."

Me: "Hmmm."

*   *   *

Higher education does exist in Vietnam. However, I've talked to very few Vietnamese who have finished high school or, for that matter, elementary school. Colleges do exist, but for the Vietnamese to attend a university is extremely uncommon. There is simply not enough money in a family for a child to spend time in school. They must help the family to survive as early as possible. Often this begins when the child is old enough to beg. The poverty cycle, of course, perpetuates itself.

*   *   *

Minh gave me one reason why her country does not progress and is in a state of economic stagnation at best.

"Very few doctor, lawyer, engineer in Vietnam," she once told me. "Boys, they go Army very young. Stay away maybe fifteen years."

As we continued our discussion, I detected a strong pride she had in the fact that her father worked to support the family. Usually a mother works while the father stays at home, when not in the army.

The Vietnam participant constantly asks, "Why?" Why has America pumped billions upon billions of dollars into Vietnam? Why has America sacrificed thousands of its own sons and daughters? Is it for the people of Vietnam? Whatever the reason, perhaps the leaders who make policy should review the basic premise of their goal. To do so would reveal that the South Vietnamese cater neither to communism nor capitalism. Their basic concern is not an abstract idea or ideal—rather it is to survive. In their overwhelming need to survive, they take on the characteristics of a greedy, hungry animal.

We, the Americans, have shown them what it is to have money. We have flaunted it in their faces, then rapidly withdrawn it. This, of course, builds up much greater frustrations and dissatisfaction than merely not having any. So these people, the Vietnamese, are doubly plagued. Not only are they members of the "have-nots" in the world, but they also have seen, and very much want, the possessions of the "haves."

At this point, the Vietnam participant asks whether the billions upon billions of dollars which America has pumped into Vietnam has brought a benefit. If so, I know not where. The people have not been given any of this money. Their main objective in life is still mere survival.

The American soldier further asks, "Why am I here? Why are we here?" It is not to protect these people from communism, as our policy-makers would have us believe. The Vietnamese, like the American soldiers here, are faced with an impossible situation. Consequently, their narrow scope does not conceive of anything other than the basic, crude instincts of man. It matters not to them who they are ruled by. Nor does nationalism play a role. Each individual is concerned only with his own well-being and existence.

Generalizations aside, my impression is that they very simply do not care about America, Americans, or our ideals. They lie to us, they cheat us, they steal from us, and in the end they kill us. As a result of this war, it is hard for us, the Americans, to remember that ultimately this is their country.

The sentence placed on every person sent to Vietnam is nothing less than exile to a forsaken land. These Americans in exile can't help questioning the wisdom of a structure which commits itself to such a ridiculous folly. The absurdity of this action is now apparent to the politicians and to the military. However, the absurdity in human terms can only be real to those who have been exiled here.

It will take much more than merely bringing the troops home to bring sanity to our world. It will take more than a token change in American priorities. But there are those, the ones who were exiled, who have seen the madness in these types of decisions and who will never again complacently accept them.

"You're not leaving here—none of us are."
—Rich, fellow soldier in Vietnam

THE MIND
Richard Pena, Winter 1972

THOUGHTS FROM THE FRONT: WHAT DAY IS THIS? IS IT SUNDAY OR Monday or maybe Saturday? What does it matter? Here, all the days are the same. What is it to live by sanity and reason? Is there any innocence left in this world? Will we, who have been exiled to this forsaken place, ever return to our homes? Will we ever again experience happiness? Will we ever again laugh? Won't somebody help us? Doesn't anybody care enough? What am I doing here? What are we dying for?

The above are questions that run through everyone's mind while in Vietnam. It's as if your mind refuses to accept the events here as real. Yet you are in Vietnam, and the bullets and bombs are very real. The deaths also are real. Continually the Vietnam participant asks why. It is all so senseless, so insane. The American soldier in Vietnam is forced to survive within this world until some higher power dictates that he can go home. We, the last ones out, have lived through the Kissinger Peace Talks of 1972. We hoped beyond all hope that a rational settlement would finally be achieved.

Of course, we did not know what to believe, having been continually misled and lied to. And when a disagreement occurred at the Peace Talks, America's response was to bomb Hanoi relentlessly with more than a hundred B-52 bomber strikes per day—the heaviest bombing of the war. During this period, the United States engaged in the heaviest aerial attack in the history of warfare on North Vietnam. We hoped it would work, but we also had our doubts.

There's a lot of time to read; to think; to theorize; to discuss priorities, foreign policy, and values; and to recognize the tragedy involved with Vietnam. Yet, to speak out about the tragedy is said to be anti-American. Despite all the Vietnam participants have endured in this forsaken country, many self-acclaimed "true Americans" call us disloyal because we speak of mistakes, of failure—because we speak the truth as we experienced it. I submit that the true American patriots are those who see the faults of our country and do not hide from them but instead attempt to rectify them.

A certain attitude begins to develop in the Vietnam participant. It is a little bit of an "I've taken your best shot; you can't hurt me" type of attitude. The soldier has had to endure and survive things that most people cannot even conceive. Back in The World, the greatest threat was that you might be sent to Vietnam—and everyone knew what might happen then. Now that you have been sent to Vietnam, a hardness of character develops. A basic distrust of institutions begins to evolve. Above all, disrespect for traditional authority develops.

What Ted Kennedy once said about his tragedies accurately describes the Vietnam participant: "There is something about me I had hoped you would understand. I can't be bruised. I can't be hurt anymore. After what's happened to me, things . . . just don't touch me, they don't get to me." This is not to say the Vietnam participants are simply calloused. However, we have developed a new perspective on life.

There is little self-deception among the Vietnam participants. The physical dangers, compounded with the mental pressures, are staggering. The physical destruction is easily seen. "Horrible" is often a mild word for describing the senseless mutilations inflicted by this war. The injuries are visible, and the repair, accordingly, is visually evident. However, the most far-reaching impact of this war is harbored in the minds of those who have been in Vietnam. These invisible pains are very real—they exist and are as costly as physical mutilations.

The mental pain in Vietnam is constant and becomes more apparent as the year-long days pass. The mental stress is inescapable. It shows in everyone. It shows in your friends, it shows in your enemies, and soon it shows in you.

People who were perfectly normal have their whole life changed by their experiences in Vietnam. Some have physical pain, but all have mental pain. It is inescapable, and it is continual. It is like an ever-increasing pressure, and the avenues for mental escape are few. It is an endurance test. No one can honestly say he likes life in this arena. One can't really live here—just exist and carry the scars home. Scars that no one else may realize are there.

The predominant emotional tone in Vietnam is dictated by the continuous absurdity and apparent madness. The absurdity creates a feeling of unreality. It is difficult to describe the mental stresses to someone who has not experienced war. To begin with, young kids are thrown into a different country, a different culture, and into what appears to be a different era. There is no justice, no logic, and often no reason for totally inhumane acts. It's as though all the values of fellowship and fair play have been thrown out the window. What was right back home is the wrong approach in Vietnam—if you want to survive. And what was wrong back home is right in Vietnam—if you want to survive.

The world is completely turned upside down, and the soldier had better adapt. Put simply, your moral system is inverted. It is madness, and it is about surviving that day. The past and your value systems are distant memories. Yet this mad world comprises your existence. It is the unreal "reality" from which there is no escape. Everyone feels that there are no honors to be won in Vietnam, there will be no honors given back home for participating in this war.

Soon a new attitude of thinking begins to develop. Extreme existentialism is not merely a vague concept, but instead a way of life. The immediate is all that matters. Memories of the past are but vague dreams; the future is light-years away. As each day passes, the hope of seeing your family and friends diminishes, as does your grasp on what reality is like in The World.

Although this situation generally prevails in the participants of any war, in Vietnam it feeds on the lies, the betrayals, and the corruption typifying this entire war. The Vietnam participant feels that he is being used, that he is but a puppet who was sent to risk his life so others can profit. Generally, the rage is directed at any symbol of official authority which can be linked with American involvement here.

The stress and pressure of Vietnam is compounded by the fact that the individual is fighting all the time and is fighting everyone around him. He must fight the Viet Cong, the North Vietnamese Army, and often the South Vietnamese, for physical survival. He must also fight the South Vietnamese people, the war profiteers, the Army, and sometimes his friends for mental survival. For 365 days the Vietnam participant must fight and fight and fight. Here, everyone is considered your enemy.

As the days pass, the bonds with sanity slowly become thinner. You are aware of what is happening, yet you can't do anything about it. You see it in yourself, and you see it in others. As days become weeks and weeks become months, the pressure of merely being in Vietnam mounts. Feelings of rage and anger begin to take over your core. Soon you are angry and bitter all the time. You wake up angry, and you go to bed angry.

A Vietnam participant who was reaching the end of his tour described it to me as follows: "It's gotten beyond the point of fighting to maintain your sanity here. All you can do is make it through alive and get your head together after you get back to The World."

Some will; some will not.

PART IV

THE FINAL FLIGHTS
John Hagan

THE JANUARY 1973 PARIS PEACE AGREEMENT PROVIDED FOR WITHDRAWAL of U.S. combat troops over a sixty-day period. However, the North Vietnamese were already massing troops to topple the South Vietnamese government. The North Vietnamese streamed bumper-to-bumper military traffic down the Ho Chi Minh Trail into the south.

Meanwhile, departure date cards were being handed out to the last American combat troops. A card bearing the date "X+1" meant that the soldier with that lucky number got to leave the next day. Richard was given card X+59—meaning he would leave on the last day permissible by the Treaty. This was later changed to X+61. Richard proudly held tight to his card, even when a friend later offered to trade. He never learned why there was a sixty-first day extending beyond the Treaty provision, but it matched his determination to be the last one out. Richard didn't want any more Americans to die for what he regarded as a misguided war.

At the same time Richard Pena left on the last plane out of Saigon, sixty-seven U.S. prisoners of war also boarded a flight from Hanoi. The North Vietnamese memorialized Richard's *Last Plane Out* in a framed picture at its War Remnants Museum. They considered this to be the day the war ended.

On March 29, 1973, the American public learned about the final flights that took Richard and the last remaining ground combat troops home from Vietnam. In a misjudgment of historic proportions, the *New York Times* gave the story "U.S. Forces Out of Vietnam" second billing to "Nixon Sets Meat Price Ceilings." A more telling headline elsewhere in the paper read, "McCord Testifies His Fellow Plotters Linked High Nixon Aides to Watergate." That story reported on Attorney General John Mitchell's guiding role in Watergate.

Today, many consider Watergate to be the defining story of the Nixon years. Narrowly remembering Vietnam as the legacy of Lyndon Johnson, most Americans have forgotten Nixon's essential involvement in the war. In fact, after the Nixon years, most of the U.S. public tried to forget that the war had happened altogether.

This phenomenon is similar to what happened with the Holocaust at the end of World War II. Americans in the middle years of the twentieth century had trouble talking about and remembering Nazi Germany's state-sponsored genocide of Jews and other ethnic groups. Elie Wiesel's memoir, *Night*, had only a small readership when it was first published in 1960, and Journalist David Halberstam's book *The Fifties* (1993) does not include a single reference to the Holocaust.

It was not until the 1993 opening of the Holocaust Museum in Washington, D.C., that Americans became truly aware of the mass murder of the European Jews. By 2007, Wiesel's *Night* sold more than ten million copies. The public has not ignored Vietnam in the same way or to the same degree as the Holocaust, but there are parallels in the way that the war's historical importance has been minimized.

Fortunately, a growing number of Americans today are revisiting the Vietnam War in new ways. In 2010, two young female authors published popular novels about the war—Marti Leimbach with *Man from Saigon* and Tatjana Soli with *The Lotus Eaters*. Although the war was fought while they were still children, their books are vivid and detailed. In the same year, Karl Marlantes, who fought in Vietnam as a marine, published his acclaimed debut novel, *Matterhorn*. Finally published when Marlantes had reached the age of sixty-five, it took him more than thirty years and much rewriting to find his readership. The publication of these books reveals a renewed interest in those forgotten final years of the war.

In his Pulitzer Prize-winning *Vietnam: A History*, Stanley Karnow wrote, "As the last Americans left Hanoi in March [1973], the prevailing sentiments in the United States were relief that the war had ended and revulsion toward the very subject of Vietnam." Karnow reported that "American news organizations closed their offices or drastically reduced their staff in Saigon, exorcising Vietnam from newspaper headlines and television screens."[22]

However, the Paris Treaty allowed a token contingent of non-combat U.S. military personnel and civilians to remain. The U.S. embassy in Saigon stayed open in a dubious display of support for the South Vietnamese government, which was clearly on its last legs. A contingent of Defense Department civilian employees stayed behind as well.

Gen. Frederick C. Weyand was the commander left behind to "furl the flag" for the last combat troops in March of 1973. *The New York Times* reported, "As the last American commander in Vietnam said goodbye to the huge white tropical building that was sometimes called Pentagon East, a force of 7,200 American civilians employed by the Department of Defense was standing under the eaves."

Two years later, North Vietnamese soldiers finally crashed through the gates to take control of the Presidential Palace in downtown Saigon. The U.S. contingent rushed to board their helicopters and barely escaped with their lives. Weyand's ceremonial role was deeply ironic; as early as 1967, he had told a CBS news correspondent of his well-known predecessor, Gen. William Westmoreland, that "Westy just doesn't get it. The war is unwinnable. We've reached a stalemate, and we should find a dignified way out."[23]

Robert McNamara said much the same thing in a private memorandum he wrote to President Johnson in 1967.[24] In his memoirs, McNamara essentially conceded that he and Westmoreland had presided over a military mistake. He concluded not only that the toll of the war was too high, but also that he himself should have urged withdrawal much earlier.

Toward the end of his life, McNamara wrote, "I believe we could and should have withdrawn from South Vietnam either in late 1963 amid the turmoil following the Diem assassination or in late 1964 or early 1965 in the face of increasing political and military weakness in South Vietnam."[25] In November of 1963 alone, seventy-eight American lives were lost in Vietnam. McNamara's reflections support the notion that ending the war sooner could have saved a huge number of lives.

In August 1967, the writer R.W. Apple published Gen. Weyand's off-the-record remarks in the *New York Times*. The article angered Westmoreland and President Johnson, who feared that it would plant seeds of doubt about the war among the American public. Weyand's trenchant views included the following observation: "I've destroyed a single division three times. I've chased main-force units all over the country, and the impact was zilch. It meant nothing to the people."

Weyand's remark echoed a refrain heard frequently in Richard's operating room and throughout Vietnam: "It don't mean nothing."

With the resumption of the bombing of North Vietnam in December 1972, President Nixon put his own desperate stamp on the war. Karnow describes the scale of Operation Linebacker II:

> Starting on December 18, B-52 and other American aircraft flew nearly three thousand sorties during the next eleven days, excluding Christmas Day, mainly over the heavily populated corridor that stretched sixty miles between Hanoi and Haiphong. They dropped some forty thousand tons of bombs in the most concentrated air offensive of the war. [26]

North Vietnam reported the bombing killed 1,318 persons in Hanoi and 305 in Haiphong. The North Vietnamese shot down fifteen

B-52s and another eleven aircraft, killing ninety-three U.S. pilots and capturing thirty-one. The North Vietnamese used the prisoners as bargaining chips once the Paris peace talks resumed.

In 1973, the *Times* estimated that—in addition to the nearly 60,000 American soldiers who died in Vietnam—the North Vietnamese military, the South Vietnamese military, and the Viet Cong altogether suffered a million deaths. The same article estimated that one million additional South Vietnamese civilians died and that the war displaced six to seven million civilian men, women, and children—nearly half of South Vietnam's population. Homes and belongings were lost or destroyed as families were scattered throughout the region.

The Vietnam War was fought much differently than World War II or the Korean War. Few of the military engagements involved frontline battles or large formations of soldiers. Instead, the U.S. and South Vietnamese military depopulated, plowed under, and defoliated large land areas, declaring them "free-fire zones" for "search-and-destroy" operations. The U.S. military carried out most of their attacks with tanks, armored cars, and helicopter gunships. If U.S. scouts spotted enemy troops, they would summon air and artillery assaults to kill the enemy while keeping their own casualties low. Over time, aerial bombings practically replaced land attacks. This method of war had a profound impact on the Vietnamese civilian population, and civilian casualties were often misidentified in the enemy body counts.

The *New York Times* called the December bombing ordered by Nixon "stone age barbarism," while the *Washington Post* called it "savage and senseless." The acts of the Nixon Administration could have suitably been categorized as war crimes. Instead, they became the basis for Kissinger's Nobel Peace Prize. In his book *Ending the Vietnam War*, Kissinger gives a vainglorious account of how he won the 1973 Noble Peace Prize for his Paris negotiations. He gives little attention to the loss of life in South Vietnam in the last years of the war, although he does reveal much about the historical and political forces that allowed casualties to mount.

It is perplexing that the American public remembers Nixon more for the pettiness of the Watergate scandal than for the destructiveness of the Vietnam War. Kissinger argued that Watergate turned Congress against Nixon and his pursuit of the war. But like the *Times* and *Post* editorial writers, the American public had lost patience with Nixon's escalation of the air war before Watergate was revealed.

"Who can ever know what your personal war involved?
You had to remain there and say good-bye to your friends one by
one until only you remained. With each good-bye, a little sanity
must have been sacrificed. In the end did loneliness reign?
Can you ever recreate Vietnam so the untraveled masses
can understand what it was actually like?"
—Bozo, Fellow Solider in Vietnam

THE LAST ONES OUT
Richard Pena, Winter 1972

WE WERE TOLD THAT A CEASE-FIRE AGREEMENT WAS TO BECOME EFFECTIVE 8:00 a.m. Sunday, January 28. "Peace," we thought. "At last."

I was awakened at 3:00 a.m. Friday morning by a knock at the door. I was needed at the hospital. Mass casualties. While the world was rejoicing over the prospect of peace in Vietnam, twenty-two rockets hit Bien Hoa Air Base. Twenty-one Americans were wounded. Mark Miller arrived in our emergency room DOA, just two days before the agreement was to take effect. He was one of the last Americans to die in Vietnam before the cease-fire actually took effect.

Hours later Da Nang got hit. More mass casualties were expected. Then within six hours Pleiku was hit. We prepared yet again for an expected onslaught of injured. The rockets had hit an enlisted men's barracks. Luck or destiny—the barracks were empty at the time.

So the war continued. Of course, the cease-fire brought us a sense of relief. On January 27, 1973, the Paris Peace Accords were signed by the participants—North Vietnam, the Viet Cong, South Vietnam, and the United States. To me, it was something of an anticlimactic victory for peace. It took so long in coming, and in the end the agreement that was reached was one of ambiguity, which contained ineffective checks.

Those of us in Vietnam, who know the people and the provisions, realized that the agreement was merely a cover for an American retreat. Indeed, what struck me about the treaty was not so much what it said as what it did not say. President Nixon saturated the world with words like "just peace," "honorable peace," "right kind of peace." The sad fact is that there is no peace in Vietnam. The fighting continues to be even more intense than ever.

In these last days of involvement, I wonder whether the world actually believes that this is anything but a retreat. The tragic thing is that this American retreat could have taken place four years ago. Of course, it would not have been laced with the words "just, honorable, etc." But then, they are phantom words which are in no way achieved through the Paris Accord. This "honorable" defeat has cost our nation more than 20,000 American lives in the last four-year period.

Although in the days following the signing of the Paris agreement, the war is classified as over, the dangers are greater than ever. In the midst of our retreat, Americans are getting massacred. It is as if some higher authority has declared open season on Americans. More Americans are meeting with serious injuries in the days immediately following the signing in Paris than during any comparable period since I arrived in Vietnam.

Everyone is after us. The South Vietnamese are turning on Americans as a vicious animal turns on its master. Confusion reigns in the greatest retreat this country has ever seen. Most flights are leaving from Tan San Nhut airfield. As a result, most Americans in country are migrating to Saigon. That is where we are making the last stand before we leave, the stand against the people who have hated us for so long. Saigon, for all practical purposes, has turned into the Dunkirk of Vietnam.

The agreement specifies that all Americans are to be out within sixty days. All American military in Vietnam have been given an X plus day on which to leave. My date of departure was initially listed as X plus 59, but subsequently I have been given a departure date of X plus 61—the very last day American troops are to withdraw from Vietnam.

There are, of course, several vital areas that need to remain open until the last day of withdrawal. The operating room is one. There are no scheduled surgeries these last days, but we always need to be ready for emergencies. The unexpected is always expected. Four operating room techs are to stay until the end: John Buydos, John Goodwin, Sau Yung, and myself. John B. and John G. have been given X plus 60. Sau and I are assigned X plus 61.

One problem troubles me: in these last days, there is no one left to cover our retreat. The infantry and most of the MPs have been sent home. The medical staff, some administrators, and some of the others remain. I accept my X day. In fact, it is preferable. The Vietnam War has been a large part of my life for seven years. It has been my entire life for eleven months. It is difficult for anyone to understand the intense emotions built up within this time. There is great satisfaction in watching all Americans leave Vietnam.

As I prepare to depart this country, my mind is weighed down by the events that have transpired in the last eleven months. No one can ever begin to understand. Leaving is not at all the way I had imagined it would be. There is not the ecstatic happiness which I had anticipated. There is no smiling, by me or by others. There is not even the lifting of a burden. In these last days before departing, I realize that the weight I have carried for the past eleven months will never be lifted from my shoulders.

In this distant and forsaken land, in these troubled times, I have seen that which wise men strive for, which cowards run from. I have seen the horrors and beauties of life in their barest form. I, too, now realize that once one has seen the truth of life, he is condemned to live in it forever.

At Last . . . At Last
Richard Pena, Spring 1972

Remember a spring day,
A soft breeze,
A gentle smile.
Remember when logic ruled decision making,
Remember?

In several days, we, the last American troops in Vietnam, will depart. The thoughts racing through my mind in these final hours are many. Eleven months is such a long time to stay in one place. In Vietnam, it is an eternity. My thoughts now increasingly turn to my home, to the people there. Faces, places, and names faded many months ago. Yet the remembrances of understanding and happiness linger in my mind. Was it but eleven months ago that I walked in those streets now forgotten? How I have aged in my exile. How can it be that I've forgotten what life was like before this war?

So another era draws to an end. What we have done in Vietnam cannot be righted. It cannot be forgiven. Perhaps someday the American people will learn how they have been manipulated and lied to. Perhaps those who rule deem it expedient to conceal the truth. I consider such deception a threat to the freedom of the American people.

Unfortunately, the impact of Vietnam on our society will not terminate with troop withdrawals. The questions which prompted the war still exist. America remains divided. Intervention, by choice, into faraway countries threatens the well-being of America. Even the political novice must be made aware that our nation must guard against any involvement similar to Vietnam.

Those Americans who have been to Vietnam will speak to you of bureaucratic decay, of destruction, of horror, of misplaced priorities, of necessities. Listen to them, for they are painfully aware of the consequences of another involvement such as this. Of all the mistakes we have made in Vietnam, the gravest would be our failure to learn from these mistakes. There must never be another Vietnam.

PART V

THE AMERICAN MEMORY
John Hagan

ONE OF THE MOST IMPORTANT REMINDERS OF THE WAR FOR AMERICANS IS the Vietnam Memorial. Built alongside the National Mall in Washington, D.C., the memorial was finished in 1982, approximately ten years after Spc. 4 Richard Pena's last flight.

Designed by artist and architect Maya Lin, the instantly recognizable V-shaped wall bears the names of 58,282 Americans who died or went missing in the war. The names are inscribed on multiple marble slabs lining a walking path. To symbolize the national wound caused by the war, the path slopes ominously downward and cuts deep into the earth before slowly rising back up to ground level. The memorial performs the contradictory task of both questioning the horrors of the war while honoring the personal courage and sacrifice of the people who died. 27

Second only to the Memorial are the movies and books that form our impressions of Vietnam. Classic fictional and non-fictional accounts by Vietnam War veterans—such as Tim O'Brien's *The Things They Carried* and Ron Kovic's *Born on the Fourth of July*—convey the drama and trauma of the conflict. Movies such as *Deer Hunter*, *Apocalypse Now*, *Full Metal Jacket*, *Coming Home*, and *Born on the*

Fourth of July etched "The Nam" and the return to "The World" in unforgettable images.

As important as these narratives are, sociologist Jerry Lembcke reveals that Vietnam War films often portray a one-sided political morality. These films typically depict the antiwar movement as being repugnant and irrational, while misrepresenting antiwar Vietnam veterans as criminal, crippled, or crazy. Members of the antiwar movement are often shown being outrageously disrespectful or hostile to Vietnam veterans. Lembcke, himself a Vietnam War veteran, argues that the contrived hostility between antiwar groups and veterans is not true to life.[28]

Coming Home (1978), remembered as one of the most antiwar Vietnam films, pits an antiwar veteran (John Voight) against another more patriotic veteran (Bruce Dern). The film contains a scene of a returning soldier (played by Dern) encountering unwelcoming demonstrators as he steps off the plane.

The 1989 film *Born on the Fourth of July* misrepresents the wheelchair-bound Ron Kovic (played by Tom Cruise) and his powerful address to the 1976 Democratic National Convention. The film does not reveal that Kovic was supporting a Gold Star Mother's vice presidential nomination of Fritz Efaw, who ran on the single platform of providing full and unconditional amnesty to all dodgers and deserters. Kovic said, "I am proud to come to this convention to represent war resisters."

One of the most enduring images of the Vietnam War is that of antiwar demonstrators spitting on returning soldiers. However, Lembcke's research revealed that these stories were based on nothing more than hearsay evidence. The myth that veterans were "spat-upon" likely began after Richard Nixon's public attacks on the antiwar movement. Fearing his internal opponents even more than the Vietnamese, Nixon castigated war protesters for their supposed disloyalty to the troops. (The Bush Administration later revived this line of argument during the Iraq War.)[29]

The myth of the "spitting protester" and animosity between veterans and protesters only spread after the war had been lost. Meanwhile, Vietnam films failed to depict the very real relationships that existed between veterans and protesters, creating version of history that was skewed against the antiwar movement. As Lembcke notes:

> . . . the story of mutually supportive relations between Vietnam veterans and the anti-war movement never made it to the screen. Except for a half dozen films in the late sixties, we seldom see veterans and the movement in the same story lines. . . . Once the war is lost, however, the frequency of references to the anti-war movement's animus toward soldiers and veterans increases. By 1977, two years after this war is actually lost, the first films portraying hostility between the anti-war movement and veterans appears.[30]

The news of the Watergate burglary dominated the headlines around the time when Richard flew home from Vietnam with the last of the ground troops. It is important to remember that the Watergate scandal was deeply tied to the Vietnam War, and that Nixon ordered the Watergate burglars to gather proof that antiwar leaders were subversives and traitors. The "Plumbers" who conducted the Watergate break-in previously had burglarized Daniel Ellsberg's psychiatrist's office in an effort to discredit his revelation of the classified Pentagon Papers.

The first efforts to impeach Nixon originally centered on his abuses of power in Vietnam. Why, then, is Nixon associated more with Watergate than Vietnam? For that matter, why does our culture remember so little about the end of the Vietnam War?

The reason is that once the Watergate narrative grabbed headlines and dominated the public attention, it overwhelmed our memories of the Vietnam War. As the Watergate storyline became swollen and distorted, the true chain of cause and effect got lost in the shuffle. As sociologist Michael Schudson notes, "almost all the memories and narratives of Watergate are distortions, omitting Vietnam or crediting its importance and then leaving it to the side. . . . indeed, the investigation of Watergate itself in 1973 and 1974 can be judged a form of forgetting Vietnam."[31]

The Watergate break-in was a response to the publication of the Pentagon Papers. Meanwhile, the first impeachment effort was made in response to Nixon's unauthorized bombings in Cambodia. However, the House of Representatives failed to impeach Nixon for the Cambodia bombings and could not get a majority to condemn him for abusing executive power. Because the Watergate scandal presented a fresh opportunity to impeach Nixon, his opponents tossed aside the old impeachment narrative in favor of a new one. As a result, history overlooked the terrible final years of Vietnam, focusing instead on a bungled robbery.

Harold Koh, the former Dean of Yale Law School, argued that investigators used a very similar logic during the Iran–Contra affair in the 1980s. The Watergate investigation focused on "what the President knew" and "when." Likewise, the Iran–Contra inquiry tried to determine how much Reagan knew about the arms-for-money deal. Again, the more important question—"How can we prevent presidential abuse of power in foreign policy?"—slipped from view.[32]

In Watergate, the official charge ultimately revolved around obstruction of justice. But because of this, the judgment of law remained silent about the abuse of American military force in Vietnam and Cambodia. This judicial silence failed to check the power of the executive branch and allowed American foreign policy to continue along frighteningly similar lines.

To truly learn from Vietnam, we must remember the war for what it was: an abuse of power in foreign relations that killed, injured, and displaced millions of people. We cannot forget this war. If we fail to acknowledge the dysfunctional political system that perpetuated it, we will forget one of the most important lessons of our nation's history. This book is one step towards reconstructing our collective memory.

Among those forgotten are the more than half-million soldiers who left the military voluntarily, the designated deserters for whom Ron Kovic spoke at the 1976 Democratic National Convention. Few today remember that when President Gerald Ford pardoned Richard Nixon for the crimes of Watergate, he tried to offset and co-opt political opposition by launching a clemency program for draft dodgers and deserters. But while Nixon received a full, free, and absolute pardon, Ford's clemency program required up to two years of alternative service and a reaffirmation of allegiance to the United States.

A Toronto newspaper editorial observed at the time that, "the president of their country offered a better deal to his predecessor who tried to destroy the democratic institutions of their country than he did to [deserters]."[33] President Jimmy Carter offered Vietnam draft dodgers a full and unconditional pardon on January 20, 1977, his first day in office, which took effect immediately. However, later, beginning on April 5, 1977, he only opened a six month-window for Vietnam deserters to return to "military control" for less-than-honorable discharge.

Of the 50,000 soldiers who went permanently AWOL during the Vietnam War, only three percent took up Ford's clemency offer, and only ten percent received Carter's pardon. Vernon Jordan, then the executive director of the National Urban League, resigned in protest from Ford's Presidential Clemency Board, explaining that, "while most of the public's attention has been focused on 50,000 or so war resisters, total amnesty should include the more than 650,000 Vietnam-era veterans who hold less than honorable discharges, which amount to lifetime penalties keeping them from government and many private sector jobs, and from rights and benefits enjoyed by other veterans."

He added, "It's time to finally end the war by declaring complete, immediate, universal, and unconditional amnesty." This amnesty never happened.

PART VI

THIRTY-SEVEN YEARS LATER
Richard Pena, 2010

MANY YEARS AGO, ALONG WITH OTHER YOUNG AMERICANS, I LEFT A small country in Southeast Asia. We were unique because we were the last of a massive evacuation by the most powerful country in the world. As I now sit at my desk, thinking about what happened in Vietnam, I also reflect on what our forefathers would say. What advice would they give us? What would they say about our war, even though it really wasn't a war because Congress never authorized it? What would they say about our country sending 3 million young men and women to a country halfway around the world for a questionable cause and a war we could not win? I think they might say, "You broke our trust; don't let it happen again."

I have been asked, "What was it like, being there for those last days? Do you still remember?" Yes, I do remember. It was a mass exodus, and only a few of us were still there by late 1972. They constantly told us that we would leave soon, and we wanted to believe it, more than anything in the world. But something would always go wrong.

To the governments in power, the Peace Talks were like a chess match, but to us they were a matter of life and death. Our hopes went up whenever we heard rumors of peace, but we were always disappointed when the talks would stall. I remember Christmas Eve, 1972. We were sitting on the porch of "the Pax," an old hotel converted into living quarters by the military. The Americans lit up the sky in celebration with our own flares—an expensive firework display for the troops. Meanwhile, there was the Christmas bombing of North Vietnam.

Carried out between December 18 and December 29, 1972, the Christmas bombing was the largest heavy bomber strike launched by the U.S. Air Force since the end of World War II. We all thought it was pointless. On New Year's Eve, the team threw a big party in the OR. Fortunately, there were no emergencies that night.

As January began, again there were rumors of peace. By this time, we were weary of having our hopes lifted up and dashed. Those of us who had lived in the villa had moved to the Pax. The Pax was still in the community and that helped us cope with some of the stress. It allowed us to pretend that everything was normal, especially when we sat outside on the porch and watched the busy street below. Instead of beach chairs overlooking the ocean, we sat in small, rickety chairs watching the people of war-torn Saigon. It was an effort just to keep our sanity. As we were either at the Pax or at the hospital for twenty-four hours a day, seven days a week, it was difficult for our minds to escape the war—even for a second.

Then came January 27, 1973, when the Paris Peace Accords were signed. Henry Kissinger and Le Duc Tho finally negotiated an agreement, and American troops were to be out in sixty days. Upon hearing this, our first reaction was skepticism. After being disappointed and lied to for so many times, we felt like scorned lovers.

The next day, our superiors at the operating room called us together. Without much discussion, they started handing out numbered slips of paper, which we called X numbers. It is important to understand that to us these numbers were life itself. We feared that all hell was about to break loose.

American troops left their equipment behind as they moved to

Saigon as quickly as possible. The plan was for our soldiers to check in at 3rd Field first before going to Tan San Nhut Airfield. From there, they were flown out in plane after plane after plane. In retrospect, our military training was indispensable. How else could thousands of people evacuate from a foreign country in a matter of two months?

When the X numbers were handed out, it was remarkable how the officers generally got the lowest numbers. But at the time, it was expected that everyone would try to save themselves. No complaints. I understood. This was war. When survival is at stake, people rush for the exit without considering those stepped on or left behind. So it was in the last days of Vietnam.

I was given X+59. "Oh, great!" I thought. "The last day." American troops were to be out in sixty days, so that meant I would leave on the second-to-last day. Later, my number was changed to X+61. I raised my hand and—with my hotshot law school training—said, "Wait a minute—this is illegal. The treaty says we are to be out in sixty days, not sixty-one."

I was told, "Soldier, you're going to turn out the lights in Vietnam."

So there I was, the little guy from San Antonio, a Spc. 4, given the honor of turning out the lights in Vietnam. "Great," I thought again, this time with a smile.

I still remember the bravery of those around me in those last days. I try to forget those who were not so brave. I remember McCalley—or at least I think it was McCalley—who offered to trade his low X number for mine. He said, "Dickie, you have a lot to live for." To this day, I consider that to be one of the bravest acts I have ever seen. None of us knew if we would live another day, much less two more months. I thanked him and declined, although I wanted to say yes.

Then things got crazy. Can you imagine someone telling you, "Leave, leave NOW"? Everything at our hospital was left behind. Towards the end, we left the Pax and were sent to barracks at Tan San Nhut Airfield. Were we, the last ones out, afraid? I don't think so. Running on adrenaline, we just wanted to get out alive. It seemed like we stayed at the one-story barracks at Tan San Nhut Airfield for a week, but it could have been more or less time. Soldiers filed in and out as airplanes landed empty and took off filled with troops, over and over again. The evacuation was very impressive to witness.

As we waited in our barracks, it occurred to me that soon there would be only three medical personnel left in Vietnam: Sau Yung, who was also an operating room tech, a nurse, and myself. This was not ideal, but it was what it was. As the days ticked down and the only remaining doctor was scheduled to depart, I approached him and said, "Doc, you can't leave. What are we going to do if there is an emergency, or if someone needs surgery?"

As he headed for the plane, he said, "You all have seen a lot of surgeries—good luck." My heart sank—this was war.

I have never prayed as much as I did during those last few remaining days. Not for myself, but that no one would need a surgery. Thankfully, no one did. To this day, neither Sau Yung nor I have been told why we were chosen to leave on the last day. But I have my suspicions.

On the last day, we awoke to typical Vietnam March weather—tropical, warm, and humid. As the last ones to leave, we had hoped and prayed for this day for so long. After all our anticipation, finally it was here. Even the X+60 group had left. Now, it was our turn. I felt no nostalgia for my time in Vietnam—only the desire to get the hell out. I was struck by the discipline and orderliness of those who remained. There was no celebrating, no high fiving, only resignation and anticipation. I felt alert and focused. We wanted this to go right.

Finally, we were told it was time to go to Tan San Nhut Airfield. "One step closer," I thought. It was midmorning. Upon arriving at the airfield, I was a little surprised at the scene before us. There were two commercial airline planes left on the runway to take us away—the last two planes out. We, the last American soldiers left in country, formed a line. Before us, lining our path to the airline, were two lines of Viet Cong and North Vietnamese soldiers.

To this day I remember exactly how I felt—the anticipation and concern. We didn't know whether they would let us board the plane or if we would be the last Americans to die in this war. To leave Vietnam, we would have to walk between rows of soldiers who looked like they had come straight from the jungle. Their faces were not at all friendly. Moreover, we had no troops to protect us should anything unexpected happen.

Before we began our procession toward the plane, we were told that a group of South Vietnamese people had stormed the gates of Tan San Nhut and were coming towards us with guns, bayonets, and anything else they could find. I still don't know why. Were they mad we were leaving? Were they mad that we had come in the first place? Who knows?

One of our soldiers looked at me and asked what we should do. After surveying the gauntlet of Viet Cong and North Vietnamese troops in front of us, I said that I would take my chances with the V.C. over the mob and that we should walk, but walk quickly. We did. It was very eerie walking between the two lines of our enemies. Of course, we had to wonder whether they would kill us or let us board the plane.

As I approached the plane, a flash bulb went off. I looked back and saw that one of the Viet Cong was holding an old camera. I remember thinking that someday it would be an important photo. Who could have guessed that it would wind up in the War Remnants Museum in Ho Chi Minh City, labeled "Last Plane Out"?

I boarded the plane along with Sau Yung and the OR nurse. It felt like the planes had swallowed us. They took off almost simultaneously, first mine, then the other. The plane rose in a steep ascent to decrease the chances of being shot down, as they always did in Vietnam. I wondered why we were making such a rapid climb when the war was supposed to be over.

I had dreamed of this day for so long. There was a time during my darkest hours in Vietnam when I did not think it would ever come. Now we were in the air. I had always pictured us having a big celebration on the plane, but the mood was just the opposite. The air was filled with weariness and resignation. I think we all knew that leaving Vietnam did not mean we had left the war. The war had consumed us; it was still inside us. We were still angry. We were still distrustful. We were still isolated. A few of the soldiers silently played a game of cards. I simply wanted to be left alone.

Eventually, we landed in California and were processed out. So many of us felt like we had been pawns in a misguided war. We all knew that the innocence we had before the war was lost forever. We respected those who had been in Vietnam because they understood. They were soldiers. We did not respect those who were playing soldier.

At the army base where I was discharged, I passed by a young rookie officer walking the other way. In the "real world," an enlisted man is supposed to salute an officer. In Vietnam, and in the hospital, we didn't salute anyone. It was pointless. So when I walked by the young officer without saluting, he started chewing me out. When I asked if he had been in Vietnam, he told me it was none of my business and demanded a salute. I knew he hadn't. As I started to walk off, he threatened to hold up my discharge until I saluted him. "Welcome back," I thought as I begrudgingly saluted him. That would be the last time I saluted someone I did not respect.

Final Reflections

There were some who were of draft age in the late 1960s who didn't go into the service or to Vietnam. Some had deferments—academic, occupational, hardship, or medical—while others joined the Reserves or left the country. Many of these men carry the guilt of not going to Vietnam with them to this day. Recently, my veteran friend Randy Borzilleri shared a cab with three men who looked like baby boomers. When Randy brought up Vietnam, each of the three was quick to point out why they did not serve. One even went so far as to show him a surgical scar on his knee. They may not have served in Vietnam, but they still feel pain and guilt.

To these legions of men, I say that most Vietnam veterans don't care whether someone served or not. We are busy dealing with our own scars and internal tortures. The war affected every member of the baby boomer generation, and we all fought battles of one kind or another. We carry the war with us every day. "Should I have served or not? Who was right and who was wrong?" Those are questions no one can answer.

But this I do know: the war is over. It ended a long time ago. We cannot undo the past, and it is time to put the guilt behind us. The Vietnamese have put the "American War of Aggression" behind them as they move their country toward a market economy. The best thing that we can do—both as individuals and as a nation—is to acknowledge, remember, and learn from the past.

We must also take care of our veterans. Many of our soldiers came home from Vietnam broken by Post-Traumatic Stress Disorder or drug addiction. Today, approximately one third of the adult homeless are veterans—and nearly half of these are Vietnam veterans. Predominantly male, they suffer from mental illness, alcohol and substance abuse, and related disorders. These Americans were not like this when they went to Vietnam as young men and women.

Instead of being treated, many ill Vietnam veterans were neglected and put out on the street. Some suffer to this day. Randy Borzilleri visited me twenty-five years after we left Vietnam. He told me that there was no one to welcome him home or give his fellow veterans help if they needed it.

We must acknowledge the sacrifices that our veterans made. Randy and I met in a Veterans of Foreign Wars Hall. Once the bartender learned we had been medics in the war, he said, "So you two were medics? Thanks."

Randy said, "It took twenty-five years to get even a simple 'thanks.'"

The day that we—the last American soldiers—finally left Vietnam should have been a historic day, honored and recognized by the country. Instead, the front-page headline of the *New York Times* read, "Nixon Sets Meat Price Ceilings."

Meat! The veterans were second to meat. They were neglected when they came home and they deserve to be remembered now.

Despite the lesson of Vietnam, we continue to send American soldiers around the globe to fight unnecessary wars that have little chance of success. These shameful ventures are incredibly costly, both financially and in terms of human life. It is time to say to America, "Wake up!" We repeat the mistakes of the past when we blindly follow the macho call to war. Make no mistake: some wars have to be fought.

But we must learn how to tell the difference between a foolish war and a necessary one.

We should learn from Vietnam before venturing into foreign lands without clear objectives or strategies for victory and exit. Our leaders must also understand that war has real consequences. 58,282 American soldiers were killed or went missing during the Vietnam War. There were an additional 350,000 combat casualties out of the 3,100,000 U.S. soldiers who served.[34] The Vietnamese government released figures in 1995 claiming 3.1 million war deaths.[35] Many more were maimed and had limbs amputated. Even today, people are still being killed by unexploded cluster bombs.

So what can be said to the families of the 58,282 American soldiers who died or went missing? After nearly four decades, they still have not forgotten. History has not judged our country kindly when it comes to the Vietnam War. To these families, the least America can do is to say, "We are sorry. Take comfort in the fact that your son or daughter is remembered as a great American. Thank you."

America is a great nation, but if we blindly follow our leaders into wars that are destined to fail, we discredit her.

LAW DAY 2010
Richard Pena, Spring 2010

IN THE SPRING OF 2010, I WAS ASKED TO BE THE KEYNOTE SPEAKER FOR the Lubbock County Bar Association's 52nd Law Day Banquet. The program coordinator asked me to come to Texas Tech Law School, which hosted the event, to speak about future challenges to the legal profession. I happily accepted the invitation.

My wife and I flew in from Austin early on the morning of the banquet. Dean Walt Huffman, a close friend of mine, gave us a personal tour of the Law School. We spent the morning walking around the campus and remembering the old times. He was very proud to show me the new additions that had gone up under his tenure. It had been a long time since I had called him "General," as he had once been the Judge Advocate General of the Army.

At noon, we met up with Walt's wife, Anne, at a local restaurant. We all reminisced about a trip we took to Russia as part of a legal delegation to St. Petersburg Law School. Just then, I noticed David Langston, the former Mayor of Lubbock, sitting a few tables away. David and his wife, Ronda, had both traveled to Russia with us and were good friends. Throughout the day, other lawyers came up and said they were looking forward to my remarks. I felt welcomed indeed.

Walt and Anne kindly picked us up about thirty minutes before the start of the banquet, and off to the Country Club we went. I was a little nervous, as I usually am before a presentation, but I looked forward to the evening. I hoped to see my old friends at the Lubbock Bar Association and make new friends as well. Thankfully, the evening did not disappoint.

The program started right on time. The Master of Ceremonies, Layne Rouse, welcomed us all to the event. He explained that President Dwight D. Eisenhower established Law Day, USA, in 1958 to strengthen the American heritage of liberty, justice and equality under the law. Three years later, Congress designated May 1st as the official date for celebrating Law Day, USA.

Layne then outlined the order of events: an Invocation, followed by the Pledge of Allegiance, the National Anthem, a Proclamation from the City by Mayor Tom Martin, awards, and then my remarks. The evening passed along quickly, and I noticed the pride and sense of accomplishment felt by those in attendance. Our meals came, awards were given, and the recipients delighted us with their stories and reminiscences.

The President of the Bar Association, Carolyn Moore, took the podium and proceeded to give one of the most eloquent and thorough introductions I have ever heard. It was her job to make me look good, and she did it well. I was both embarrassed and proud. After everything I had been through, all the ups and the downs, I was being recognized and asked to share my thoughts with members of the profession I love.

President Moore spoke about my time as a star athlete in high school, how I was drafted and sent to Vietnam after my first year of law school, my life as an operating room specialist at 3rd Field Hospital in Saigon, and my departure from Vietnam on the very last day. She summarized my return to the States to complete law school at the University of Texas and my work practicing law in Austin.

She continued on, mentioning that I had been President of the State Bar of Texas, the American Bar Foundation, and of my local Bar

Association. She certainly had done her homework. But as she spoke, my mind drifted. I began to remember how things were not always as they were that night. I remembered, as if it were yesterday, coming back from Vietnam as a very angry young man.

Did my experience in Vietnam contribute to my accomplishments after the war? I can say that it gave me the courage, willpower and confidence to stand up against injustice and fight for my clients. It drives me to fight on behalf of average citizens against big corporations and insurance companies with massive resources. I take on many of these cases knowing that I won't receive any compensation. I continue to tell the students who work for me that it is not about the money; it is about doing what is right.

While I watched Carolyn introduce me, it felt as if the volume was gradually being turned down lower in my head. I allowed myself to think back in time to the early days of my practice. I remembered hanging my law license in the back room of my duplex and declaring myself open for business. I had started on my own, not working for any other firm or agency. It was the road less traveled, but it was my road.

I remembered the two dress shirts, suit, and pair of shoes that my parents had bought for me, which served as my "lawyer wardrobe." Without a receptionist or legal secretary, I remembered putting clients on hold before picking up again and introducing myself.

I remembered making house calls to clients because I didn't have an office. I had an old yellow car with no air-conditioning, the driver's door tied shut with a rope. I would park my beloved wreck of a car down the street from the client's house, climb out of the passenger side, and march out with my briefcase. I didn't want my clients to know I didn't have a big fancy office, nor did I want them to see my leaky, beat-up car. Clients, I thought, want their lawyers to be rich and famous.

As the President was winding up her remarks, my wife noticed that I was daydreaming. She gave me a gentle kick from under the table, bringing me back to reality just as President Moore said, "Tonight, please welcome, as your keynote speaker, Richard Pena, a friend to lawyers and a friend to those in need. A lawyer who fights the good fight."

I scrambled to make myself neat and gather my notes. But my mind had not yet completely returned from its journey into the past. As I approached the stage, I remembered being on one of the last planes out of Saigon.

I began my remarks: "Thank you, President Moore. I am pleased and honored to be with you tonight. I have been asked to talk about the future of the legal profession and the challenges that we will be facing. But before we talk about the future, it is important that we talk about the past. It is important that we remember our history and acknowledge our successes and failures, both as a profession and as a country. There is a saying—that I carried with me in Vietnam—that summarizes this widely applicable yet simple notion: 'Of all the mistakes we have made in the past, the gravest would be our failure to learn from them.'"

NOTES

1 Beverly Burr, "History of Student Activism at the University of Texas at Austin (1960-1988)" (Thesis paper, University of Texas at Austin, 1988), 46.

2 Ibid., 48.

3 Todd Gitlin, *The Sixties: Years of Hope, Days of Rage* (New York: Bantam Books, 1993).

4 Ibid., 417-418.

5 Robert McNamara, *In Retrospect: The Tragedy and Lessons of Vietnam* (New York: Times Books, 1995), xvi.

6 Henry Kissinger, *Ending the Vietnam War: A History of America's Involvement In and Extrication From the Vietnam War* (New York: Simon & Schuster, 2003), 11.

7 Lam Quang Thi, *Hell in An Loc: The 1972 Easter Invasion and the Battle that Saved South Viet Nam* (Texas: University of North Texas Press, 2011), 218.

8 Ibid., 218

9 Henry Kissinger, *Ending the Vietnam War: A History of America's Involvement In and Extrication From the Vietnam War* (New York: Simon & Schuster, 2003), 267.

10 Ibid., 287.

11 Ibid., 288.

12 Ibid., 272, 273, 288.

13 Ibid., 324.

14 Ibid., 364.

15 Ibid., 411.

16 Graham Greene, *The Quiet American* (New York: Viking Press, 1956), 144.

17 "Déjà vu Vietnam," http://dejavuvietnam.net.

18 John Ketwig, *And a Hard Rain Fell: A G.I.'s True Story of the War in Vietnam* (New York: Macmillan, 1985), 4.

19 Ibid., 135

20 Elizabeth Norman, *Women at War: The Story of Fifty Military Nurses Who Served in Vietnam* (Pennsylvania: University of Pennsylvania Press, 1990).

21 John Ketwig, *And a Hard Rain Fell: A G.I.'s True Story of the War in Vietnam* (New York: Macmillan, 1985), 180-181

22 Stanley Karnow, *Vietnam: A History* (New York: Penguin Books, 1997), 670.

23 William Grimes, "Frederick C. Weyand, Vietnam Commander, Dies at 93," *New York Times*, February 13, 2010.

24 McNamara, *In Retrospect*, 269.

25 Ibid., 320.

26 Karnow, *Vietnam*, 667.

27 Wagner-Pacifici, Robin, and Barry Schwartz. "The Vietnam Veterans

Memorial: Commemorating a Difficult Past. *American Journal of Sociology* 97 no. 2 (September 1991): 376-420.

28 Jerry Lembcke, *The Spitting Image: Myth, Memory, and the Legacy of Vietnam* (New York: New York University Press, 1998).

29 Ibid., 8-9.

30 Ibid., 9.

31 Michael Schudson, *Watergate in American Memory: How We Remember, Forget, and Reconstruct the Past*, (New York: Basic Books, 1992), 220.

32 Harold Koh, *The National Security Constitution: Sharing Power after the Iran-Contra Affair* (New Haven, Yale University Press 1990) p. 5

33 "A TOUGH CHOICE FOR EXILES," Toronto Globe and Mail, 17 September 1974, p. A3.

34 James F. Dunnigan & Albert A. Nofi. *Dirty Little Secrets of the Vietnam War*. (New York: St. Martin's Press, 2000), 240.

35 Charles Hirschman, Samuel Preston, Vu Manh Loi. Vietnamese Casualties During the American War: A New Estimate. *Population and Development Review*, Volume 21, Issue 4 (Dec., 1995), 783-812.

ABOUT THE AUTHORS

Richard Pena pointing to himself getting on one of the last planes of Americans to leave Vietnam. Photo entitled "Last Plane Out." War Remnants Museum, Ho Chi Minh City (Saigon), 2003.

RICHARD PENA served in Vietnam as an Operating Room Specialist for the United States Army. He was awarded the National Defense Service Medal, the Army Commendation Medal and the Vietnam Service Medal. Richard is now a practicing attorney in Austin, Texas. He is the former President of the American Bar Foundation and State Bar of Texas and served on the Board of Governors of the American Bar Association. While leading a legal delegation trip to Vietnam he recognized himself in a photo titled *Last Plane Out* hanging in the Ho Chi Minh City's War Remnants Museum. Seeing this photo inspired Richard to reread the journal he kept during the war, which would eventually become the heart of *Last Plane Out of Saigon*. This is his first title.

JOHN HAGAN is the John D. MacArthur Professor of Sociology and Law at Northwestern University and Co-Director of the Center of Law & Globalization at the American Bar Foundation in Chicago. He has published nine books and more than 150 articles in nationally renowned magazines and journals. His most recent book is *Who Are the Criminals?: The Politics of Crime Policy in the Age of Roosevelt and the Age of Reagan* (Princeton University Press, 2010).